DO WE NEED A BILL OF RIGHTS?

Edited by
Professor C. M. Campbell

Do We Need a Bill of Rights?

Temple Smith · London

First published in Great Britain in 1980
By Maurice Temple Smith Ltd
37 Great Russell St, London WC1

© 1980 C.M.Campbell, Lord Hailsham, Lord Scarman,
R.J.Lawrence, Lord Wade, Lord Boston, P.Wallington,
M.Robinson, K.Boyle, T.Carlin, Lord Melchett, P.Hewitt,
B.Garrett, J.Smythe, C.–D.Ehlermann, J.E.S.Fawcett

ISBN 0 85117 205 9

Typeset in 11 point Times
by Robcroft Ltd, London
Printed in Great Britain by
Billing & Sons Ltd
Guildford, London, Worcester & Oxford

CONTENTS

Preface
The Right Hon. Lord Hailsham of St Marylebone

Introduction

CONTENTS CONTINUED OVERLEAF

Editor

Professor C. M. Campbell, Faculty of Law, The Queen's University of Belfast

Contributors

The Rt Hon. Lord Scarman OBE, Lord of Appeal in Ordinary

Professor Emeritus R. J. Lawrence

The Lord Wade

The Lord Boston of Faversham

Professor Peter Wallington, Department of Law, University of Lancaster

Senator Mary Robinson SC

Professor Kevin Boyle, National University of Ireland, Galway

Mr Terry Carlin, Northern Ireland Officer, Irish Congress of Trades Unions

The Lord Melchett, Former Minister of State, Northern Ireland Office

Ms Patricia Hewitt, General Secretary, National Council for Civil Liberties

Mr Brian Garrett, Solicitor

Mr John Smythe, Special Advisor to the Secretary General, Council of Europe

Dr Claus-Dieter Ehlermann, Director General, The Legal Service, Commission of the European Communities

Professor J.E.S. Fawcett, President, European Commission of Human Rights

Acknowledgements

The articles in this book are based on contributions to the proceedings of a Conference arranged by the Standing Advisory Commission on Human Rights in Northern Ireland. I wish to acknowledge with gratitude the great co-operation shown by all the distinguished speakers in helping to prepare their original papers for publication. I also wish to thank all those others who participated in the Conference – in particular the Lord Mayor of Belfast, Councillor W. B. Bell, Dr Garrett Fitzgerald, Sir Francis Valet and Mr Brendan Kiernan. Mr Roy Jenkins, President of the European Economic Community, gave invaluable encouragement in the arrangements leading to the Conference.

I also wish to express my gratitude to fellow members of the Commission and to Mr Lionel Jacobs and Mr Peter Waterworth of its Secretariat. Miss Hazel Mount deserves, and has, my deepest thanks for assisting in the production and typing of the entire book.

Finally, the most important acknowledgment should be given to Lord Plant of Beneden CBE, the Chairman of the Standing Advisory Commission on Human Rights. His work and assistance to all members of the Commission has been considerable. If the Commission can now take the debate about the introduction of a Bill of Rights for the United Kingdom further – or in any way ensure the better protection of human rights – he can take much of the credit.

C. M. Campbell

Preface

I am delighted to commend this splendid and representative collection of essays sponsored by the Northern Ireland Standing Advisory Committee on Human Rights whose work in this field has already proved as invaluable as it has become well known.

The particular relevance of the debate to Northern Ireland is manifest. But the truth is that the underlying problems extend to the whole of the United Kingdom and must be seen there in the context of our adherence to the European Convention on Human Rights and our acceptance of the right of individual petition.

Some of the contributions provoke the question whether a separate Bill of Rights is of more than marginal significance without a corresponding entrenchment in a written constitution. It is also important to appreciate the relationship between a reception of the Convention into the domestic law of the United Kingdom and the rules of statutory interpretation by which in the course of years judges in our national courts have come to feel themselves bound. It is natural too that the question should be raised whether, in the absence of a general law extending throughout the United Kingdom, an Act specifically limited to the six counties of Northern Ireland might not itself contribute to the solution of the problems of the Province. For myself I think it would, although I would prefer broader approach.

I would also respectfully agree with those who take the unanimous view of the House of Lords Select Committee that the enumeration of the rights to be entrenched is no longer really an open question. It is surely the European Convention, as it may be enlarged and revised from time to time, or nothing. A country cannot live with two Bill of Rights. There can only be one set of entrenched provisions.

A more esoteric question concerns the European Community. If the members individually adhere to the Convention, has the Community as such a useful separate role to play?

For those who wish to know the arguments this collection of essays must prove an invaluable aid to study. I wish it every success, both for reading by the academic student and with the general public.

Lord Hailsham of St Marylebone

Introduction

Historically, the rights of individuals in the United Kingdom have been defined by judicial rulings and Acts of Parliament. The various rights, freedoms and duties of citizens are to be culled from the accumulated decisions of the courts or, where the need for broader legal control or law reform had been recognized, from statutory provisions which express the will of the sovereign parliament. The unique relationship and interplay between judge-made law and legislation evolved slowly and there are always further instances where pragmatic adjustments to the relationship continue to be made. The combinations of the courts and parliament in protecting rights and defining freedoms, has not only been defined as indigenous to Britain – it has also been claimed as an essential bulwark to democracy and to the society itself. Yet notes of scepticism have been sounded and in recent years dissatisfaction with the conventional methods of protecting rights has been expressed. There have been calls for a more radical approach and for far-reaching reforms. There is now a debate about the adequacy of the legal and political safeguards afforded the ordinary citizen, and the most important question posed is 'Do we need a Bill of Rights?'.

The purpose of this book, prepared with the current debate in mind, is to examine the best answer that can be given to this question. Some of the contributors argue for a Bill of Rights – and others against; different permutations and justifications are suggested. Many of the contributors have played a leading part in the recent debate in Britain, while others bring comparative knowledge of relevant developments elsewhere which have already influenced the legal and constitutional practices in Britain. But the articles, separately and together, are intended to allow a general and open appraisal of the issues that are involved. A serious error would be made if arguments about a Bill of Rights were confined to constitutionalists, academic specialists, or even the Members of Parliament who, as legislators, are most likely to decide on the parameters for law reform. There are, of course, a series of technical and subsidiary problems in introducing any constitutional measure where technical expertise is demanded.

Introduction

But the call for a Bill of Rights poses more than mere legalistic questions or matters of esoteric detail. It amounts to a demand for a different and more positive endeavour to be made in stating and guaranteeing the basic rights of all members of society. As such it constitutes an issue for public discussion as important as any on the political agenda.

A Bill of Rights can come in many hues and guises – this much is clear from the collection of articles. At root, however, any Bill of Rights is possessed of some characteristics or attributes which sets it apart from the traditional laws passed or legal procedures adopted in Britain. A Bill of Rights articulates the basic values that must be recognised in law as above all others. It insists that certain rights and priviledges must be afforded to all individuals – rights which are so vital (to the individuals or to the society itself) that they may not be detracted from by mundane pressures or exigencies. Such rights may be broadly stated and the reciprocal obligations on which they depend may require to be spelled out carefully. Yet these rights are, as soon as the Bill of Rights is accepted, taken as transcending all other goals or priorities or aspirations. A Bill, being of paramount status, then allows that where it is thought there has been any infringment of its Rights there should, for this reason alone, be ready access to a court for a ruling or decision.

Stated thus broadly a Bill of Rights promises much – perhaps too much. Opponents of a Bill of Rights argue that the implications of adopting such a new method of protecting rights would ill suit the legal and constitutional practices developed so painstakingly over the centuries in Britain. The sovereignty of parliament, as we understand it today, is the cornerstone of democratic government. A Bill of Rights would be anomalous, resulting in uncertainty, or, if it is to have a chance of working properly, deserves to be introduced only along with other changes amounting to a new, more or less ambitious, constitutional settlement. Either way the current debate about a Bill of Rights is crucial. Its resolution will help to shape the proper relationships which should pertain between all individuals, between individuals and groups, and between the people and the state. It should define the social, legal and political freedoms which are possible and desirable in an advanced and industrialised society where the rate of change and challenges to government appear to grow daily. It will determine the role and relevance of law in the years to come.

Since this is not a narrowly technical book the articles range widely. Some account of the increasing interest in a Bill of Rights for Britain is provided in the five articles of Part I. The last fifteen years have seen many attempts to introduce Bill of Rights in parliament and multitudinous pressure groups, interest groups and political parties have published their proposals. Yet the major development has been the emerging consensus that if there is to be such a Bill it should, following the reasoning of the Standing Advisory Commission on Human Rights and of the House of Lords Select Committee on a Bill of Rights, be by incorporating the substantive parts of the European Convention on Human Rights.

The United Kingdom is, of course, a signatory to the European Convention. Over the last decade increasing familiarity with the Convention has grown from the publicity given to cases where the United Kingdom was a party to the proceedings before the European Commission or the European Court of Human Rights in Strasbourg. Equally the central relevance of legal developments in continental Europe was underlined by the accession to the European Economic Community. Because of its intrinsic merits, its existing impact on domestic law and the value of promoting harmonisation with neighbouring countries, it is suggested adoption into domestic law of the European Convention is the best way of proceeding. An outline of salient developments which are likely in the future to continue to affect domestic law is given in Part III of the book. This part has regard to both the European Convention itself and to the contemporary thinking of the European Community as it also seeks to underwrite and protect the rights of citizens throughout Europe.

Part II contains two substantive chapters. The first should remind all of us of the proximate experience in Ireland in introducing protected rights in a written constitution onto a common law system; yet it also reiterates that *no* document by itself can guarantee the enjoyment of rights if it receives insufficient support or suffers intimidating opposition – through violence, war or insurgency for example. The second contains 'debate within a debate' as the lessons to emerge from Northern Ireland in its fraught history are examined. The seemingly in-

Introduction

tractable problems of Northern Ireland during the continuing violence and terrorism have sorely tested the adequacy of law, its methods and integrity. It is probably not an exaggeration to say that 'the troubles' in Northern Ireland have, for many people, lent particular urgency to consideration of a Bill of Rights. For people in Northern Ireland the rights and freedoms, lifestyles and privileges, taken for granted in most western countries have been regularly suspended during the past decade or totally destroyed. In this discussion there is some agreement that a Bill or Charter of Rights is required for Northern Ireland; but no-one with any experience of the situation holds to any naive assumption either that such a measure would end the continuing violence or that rights can be discussed without careful attention to associated duties and obligations.

The coverage of this book is then wide as well as general. It ranges over social, legal, political and constitutional considerations. It examines the recent history of violence and terrorist attacks on established institutions and on democracy, to seek to identify the proper stance of law and how the rule of law may best be maintained. It scrutinises developments in Strasbourg and Luxembourg to ensure the international obligations on this country the activities of partner states are not ignored. It continues the debate about the adequacy of traditional legal procedures. All these areas are relevant and come together, in considering whether there should now be a Bill of Rights and, if so, what form it should take. The various contributors of articles have gone to pains to ensure their views are expressed clearly – where they agree and where they disagree with one another is manifest. The important next step is for the debate to be widened even further. Each of us, at different times, may wish to engage in novel activities, public or private, exercise options, change habits, or make calls on government or parliament. The answer given to the question Do We Need a Bill of Rights? will profoundly influence the possibilities open to us just as it will determine our obligations under law.

Professor C. M. Campbell

Part I

THE BILL OF RIGHTS DEBATE

The adequacy of the law of the land in protecting rights – and imposing civic responsibilities and duties – has been challenged over the years. Specific reforms and changes have been suggested and some implemented. Recently there has been a demand for a more radical change – a change of method and a change of direction. There is a call for a Bill of Rights.

Over the years different attempts to introduce Bills of Rights have been made. Now the debate is seriously under way. It is firmly on the agenda for political and public debate. The articles in this Part of the book represent the major arguments for and against a Bill of Rights.

Lord Scarman places the debate within the context of law's role in modern society and the responses required of it if it is to fulfil its purposes. Professor Lawrence, more sceptically, suggests measures other than a Bill of Rights are necessary – instead of or in addition to such a Bill. In recent years Lord Wade has played a leading part in stimulating the current debate: he served on the House of Lords Select Committee which decided, by a narrow majority, that there should be a Bill of Rights for the United Kingdom. The Bill which Lord Wade successfully steered through the House of Lords is included in this Part. In spite of the decision of the Select Committee and the passage of Lord Wade's Bill through the Lords, the opposition to this measure, and the arguments deployed, are firmly presented by Lord Boston of Faversham. The concluding paper by Professor Wallington reveals how complicated and far-reaching the implications may be if the technical design of a Bill is not carefully considered. Together the papers provide an expert introduction to, as well as a continuation of, the debate about a Bill of Rights in the United Kingdom.

HUMAN RIGHTS: THE CURRENT SITUATION

Lord Scarman

Part I

It is fitting that we should assemble in Northern Ireland to discuss human rights. It is also right that we should remember that it was twenty-seven years ago that the United Kingdom accepted the international obligation to ensure that everybody in the United Kingdom should have the rights and freedoms set forth in the European Convention on Human Rights. Yet we remain one of the few signatories not to have incorporated the Convention into our own municipal law. Discussion of human rights in Northern Ireland is vital – for at least two very important reasons.

First, Northern Ireland is the one part of the United Kingdom where the imperious needs of security provide a daily challenge to the maintenance of our human rights. In Northern Ireland, our idealistic professions of virtue can be judged against the evidence of what we, in fact, do. Here our ideals are daily put to the ultimate test of action. The specific problem in Northern Ireland is to resolve the conflict of principle which arises when, in time of emergency, the law is required to reconcile liberty with security. This reconciliation has to be sought by the police, the judges, and the legislature continuously. It arises for daily decision by the police in numberless interrogations, and for judges as they handle their daily case load. So much for the first reason.

But secondly, by meeting in Belfast, we can demonstrate our admiration for what is being achieved by those responsible in Northern Ireland. I would single out for especial praise the assiduous work of the judges and the remarkable achievements of the Northern Ireland Standing Advisory Commission on Human Rights. The cynic could say that the Commission is a watch-dog, whose task is to bark against that intruder, *Injustice*, if and when any of the three arms of Government, i.e. the judicial, administrative, or executive power, puts a foot wrong. But the watch-dog can also bark to welcome home its master, *Justice*. I commend to your attention Paragraphs 13 to 15 of the *Fifth Annual Report (1978–9)*[1] of the Standing Advisory Commission. Section 8 of the Northern Ireland (Emergency Provisions) Act 1978 provides by subsection (2) that

> if, in any . . . proceedings (for a scheduled offence) where the prosecution proposes to give in evidence a statement made by the accused, prima facie evidence is adduced that the accused was subjected to torture or to inhuman or degrading treatment in order to induce him to make a statement, the court shall, unless the prosecution satisfies it that the statement was not so obtained . . . exclude the statement.

Some have been misled, by this incorporation in the statute of a fragment of the European Convention on Human Rights, into believing that, since not every 'roughness of treatment' such as 'slaps or blows of the hand on the head or face' constitutes inhuman or degrading treatment, the statute permits violence short of 'degrading treatment' in the interrogation of a suspect. But the judges have not been misled. They have interpreted the provision not as a substitution for the common law but as an additional reinforcement. To quote the Commission (paragraph 15):

> they (the judges) have taken the view that this standard is by itself too low to ensure the proper administration of justice. To the extent that the courts have gone beyond the literal interpretation of the statute they have used judicial discretion to achieve this.

This is high praise, indeed. But I would add a rider of some importance. The judges have not used their discretion in the sense that they had a choice between two courses. They have done their duty by interpreting the statute according to its legislative purpose. Parliament never intended to alter the common law, which makes it unlawful for the police to use or threaten violence during interrogation. The section merely adds a further safeguard by reference to a minimum international standard.

Incidentally, the problems arising on this subsection illustrate neatly the dangers of piecemeal incorporation into our law of bits of the European Convention on Human Rights – whether by statute or, as we have done in the English Court of Appeal, by judicial decision. Northern Ireland thus provides us with evidence as to the desirability of including within the law not only detailed legislation safeguarding specific human rights, but a *comprehensive* charter of our rights so formulated that it sets minimum standards which must be met in the absence of a specific rule covering the case, and which at the same time provides a basis of principle upon which detailed law may be constructed by legislation or by judicial decision, or by a combination of the two. For the judges do need a basis of principle upon which to approach the vital task in the twentieth century of interpreting and applying legislation. If it can be given to us by Parliament, so much the better.

Yet it is the opportunity of saluting the Standing Advisory Commission on Human Rights for its contribution to the cause of a modern Bill of Rights for the whole of the United Kingdom which makes our gathering here appropriate – perhaps even momentous. In the glorious language of the *Book of Common Prayer*, it is 'very meet, right, and our bounden duty' to give thanks and praise for the Commission's outstanding Report–*The Protection of Human Rights by law in Northern Ireland*[2], presented to Parliament in November 1977. I regard it as far and away the best study of Human Rights (not only in Northern Ireland but in the United Kingdom as a whole) yet produced in the English language. We are fortunate, therefore, to be meeting in Northern Ireland and to be participating in discussions in a context where the surrounding tragedy of human division stands as an awesome reminder of the importance of the matters at issue.

Part II

My main object in this paper is to stimulate discussion on the *two* points which require consideration if the United Kingdom is to be persuaded to adopt, as I believe it should, a Bill of Rights having statutory force in all parts of the Kingdom. The two basic questions, to which the Northern Ireland Standing Advisory Commission on Human Rights addressed its climacteric report, remain to be answered. They are:

1 Does the United Kingdom need a Bill of Rights? If the

answer is 'yes',
2 Will the European Convention on Human Rights meet the
   need?

As to the first question I will not repeat the arguments so
cogently expressed by the Standing Commission in its Report.
But I would remind you that they have prevailed in the House of
Lords to the extent that Lord Wade's Bill has passed all its stages
and now awaits – somewhat forlornly – support in the House of
Commons. It is significant that the real opposition to a Bill of
Rights comes from the party-controlled House of Commons. It
indicates the nature of the true resistance to the judicial
protection of human rights. It is fear of judicial power to curb or
review legislation. The fear is groundless. Does one observe any
panic in the Congress in the United States of America, or in the
legislatures of the Federal Republic of Germany, of the Republic
of Ireland or of India? Yet the power exists in all those states. As
always, those who have the power resist any restraint upon its
exercise, even though the restraint be designed not to restrict the
exercise, but to prevent the abuse, of power.

Current events have not, I submit, undermined the reasoning
of the Standing Advisory Commission's Report. Indeed the
more acute become our difficulties with law and order, and with
the claims of minorities, the stronger is the case for establishing
and declaring in simple, general terms, the basis of principle
upon which we intend to tackle them. However, I propose to deal
with only two of our many problems in this field. No doubt
subsequent discussions will – and I hope this is the case – cover
many of the other issues and problems. I will consider contempt
of court, and illegal immigration.

Freedom under the law is, and has been for 300 years, the
basis of our constitution and the legal system. We require no
revolution to secure it: only a reform to maintain it effectively in
our complex twentieth century society. The common law is not
an inexhaustible source of principles. There is difficulty in
adapting it so that it may operate to safeguard individuals
aggrieved by the intrusive power of government departments
administering, centrally and locally, the various sectors of the
welfare state. The judges lack guide-lines to direct them in the
handling of administrative law, or public law, as I would like to
think of it. An essentially private law system, such as that of the

common law, needs the help of a 'charter of rights' if the judges are to cope with the welfare state. Sometimes, the common law points the wrong way – or, at least, the judges think it does, which under our system is another way of saying the same thing.

Take the example of the *Sunday Times* Contempt of Court case decided by the European Court of Human Rights on 26 April 1979. As formulated by some members of the House of Lords in that case[3], English law contains a rule that it is not permissible to prejudge issues in pending proceedings. As the European Court points out, this is an altogether too inflexible and absolute rule, if freedom of speech is to be protected in the many cases where no harm could conceivably be done by pre-trial publication. Their Lordships, however, were led to such a formulation not through any failure to balance the conflicting public interests of freedom of speech and the administration of justice – indeed they were assiduous to strike the balance – but because they had to make some sort of sense of a doctrine, contempt of court, which originated in ancient and very different times. Indeed, if it did not happen to exist in our law, no one today would think of creating it. As Lord Salmon said in his evidence to the Phillimore Committee[4], when asked at what point in pending proceedings the law of contempt became effective to prevent publication of matter relevant to the issues of the case:

> Nowhere, because I would not have any contempt. I say never. Certainly never in a judge-alone case. I think the law of libel takes care of anything you may say about a civil case, and if a judge is going to be affected by what is written or said he is not fit to be a judge.[5]

It can be said that the presence of this historic doctrine in our law coupled with the absence of any Bill of Rights provision, which could subject the doctrine to the sort of considerations which Lord Salmon in his evidence, and the European Court of Human Rights in their decision envisaged, diverted the House of Lords, our supreme court, from the correct approach to the problem posed by the conflict between the freedom of the press and the administration of justice. There is, or should be no choice, as the European Court recognised, between conflicting principles. There should be one basic principle – freedom of speech – which is subject to certain exceptions. The court's true task is to define these exceptions, and to refuse to restrain freedom of speech unless the case falls clearly within one or more of them. Had the House of Lords had the advantage of a modern Bill of Rights, it would not have been led into the formulation of a principle (prejudging the issue) which the European Court believed to be unconditionally stated and unnecessary in a democratic society. And there would have been room for the application of Lord Salmon's robust common sense in all but the truly exceptional cases.

It is not only the judges, however, who need the help of a Bill of Rights – Parliament and Government do as well. Take the recent controversy over the proposed new rules for controlling entry of immigrants into the United Kingdom. The need for effective control is, of course, a matter of policy, upon which judges are not the appropriate commentators. But ways and means of exercising control can raise questions of human rights, which it *is* the duty of the courts to protect. Personal liberty and physical integrity are well protected by our law, for example by *habeaus corpus* and the criminal law. Family life, privacy, and freedom from discrimination on grounds of sex, race, colour, or national origin are not. No doubt, the judges and Parliament are moving the law in the right direction: but there is no declaration of principle comparable with Articles 8 and 14 of the European Convention on Human Rights. Had such a general principle been enacted in our law and not left to be inferred from detailed legislation regulating family life and restricting racial and sexual discrimination, I doubt whether Parliament would have been asked to confirm an immigration rule which, in pursuit of its legitimate aim of controlling immigration, will discriminate between the sexes (and between members of the same sex) in its impact upon the private lives of persons resident in the United Kingdom.

These two specific problems suggest, therefore, that current events are underlining the need for a Bill of Rights. The arguments of the Northern Ireland Report on *The Protection of Human Rights by Law* are being reinforced by later experience.

If the answer to the first question 'Does the United Kingdom need a Bill of Rights?' is answered in the affirmative, we can turn to the second question 'Will the European Convention on Human Rights meet the need?' I shall not repeat the case already made on the floor of the House of Lords, in the Standing Advisory Commission's Report, and by others for incorporating the first section of the Convention into our municipal law. There are difficulties, as the President of the European Commission Professor Fawcett has reminded us.[6] But they can be overcome; and they do not seem to have presented insuperable problems to our partners in the Common Market whose municipal law already incorporates the Convention.

Two general features of the Convention are, I think, worth emphasising: especially as little reference is made to them in the United Kingdom. First, it is a European declaration. As such, its incorporation into our law would promote the harmonisation of our laws with those of our neighbours, allies and Common Market partners. We are, with them, the direct heirs of a European civilisation springing from Greece and Rome. The Convention was drafted as a statement of universal values (to which the United Nations had declared their commitment) to be protected in Europe against the insidious internal undermining of human rights which led to the Second World War. To incorporate it into our law can only strengthen our heritage, the liberal European tradition over which we, with others, stand guard.

Second, the Convention now has the benefit of a distinguished jurisprudence developed by the European Court of Human Rights. It would be invidious in a short paper to single out decisions for special mention. But the *Golder* case [7], the case of *Ireland v. U.K.*[8], the *Klass* case[9], and the *Sunday Times* case illustrate in their different ways the tremendous assistance our judges could derive from the Convention case law. Significantly, this case law covers the 'grey areas' of English law, notably the rights of prisoners, privacy, family life, the right to be informed as well as the right to speak and to impart information. I will say no more than that there is here a quarry from which I would expect United Kingdom judges to mine pure gold. They have the outlook, the tradition, and the historical background. Why deny them the help of a weapon which, if not as modern as it might be, is kept in such good condition by a European court which has shown a profound respect for the national legal systems of the states which are parties to the Convention as well as a deep understanding of the Convention itself?

I, therefore, would answer both the questions which I have

posed in the affirmative. All I have sought to do is to illustrate from some current problems that the case for a Bill of Rights remains a strong one. We should not abandon it merely because it strikes an unfamiliar chord in the world of common law. Its music is, in truth, well suited to the themes with which our law has always been concerned.

RIGHTS AND REMEDIES

Professor R. J. Lawrence

Does the United Kingdom need a new Bill of Rights? Which rights should it contain? What changes in institutions and attitudes would it require? In this paper I shall glance at these three questions.

In doing so I take it that proponents of a British Bill of Rights want more than a pious declaration. If rights are to be taken seriously, they need to be enforceable and universal. They must be upheld by independent courts of law, binding on all persons and institutions, and supported by public opinion. An effective bill of rights, like a constitution of which it often forms part, is a higher law to which *all* are subject – from the legislators to the man in the street. In fact, this ideal of the predominance of law is a leading feature of the liberal-democratic State which has evolved during the past century or so. 'Democratic' is often used as a term of praise or approval for both democratic and liberal values, but this usage is a source of confusion. A liberal State is one in which power, especially public power, is defined and limited. In the development of liberalism, which preceded democracy, the powers of government were restricted by general and ascertainable principles. A democratic State is, roughly, one in which all can vote but the majority rule. Both liberalism and democracy entail rights, but these may conflict because the rights of a minority or an individual may be incompatible with rights claimed by a majority. This has implications which I take up later.

The first question posed is whether the United Kingdom needs an enforceable Bill of Rights binding on all persons and institutions, including Parliament? It has often been argued that the power of public authorities and of some private bodies – notably trades unions – has increased and needs to be brought under closer control. Of governmental power I need say little. Reforms beginning about 1870, and accelerated after 1945, were intended to improve welfare by providing services and regulating conduct on a massive scale. We have had torrents of legislation (often reversed or amended by successive Parliaments) and floods of regulations enforced by armies of officials, often entrusted with wide discretion. Because of our peculiar constitutional development, all this took place without adequate checks. The United Kingdom has no constitution – at least, none in the liberal sense of a body of rules that bind the legislature. Whatever Parliament enacts is law; and Parliament for most purposes means the party with most seats in the House of Commons, whether or not it has won most votes at a general election. Nor, until quite recent years, had we adequate means to control the Executive, whether by a Bill of Rights as in the United States, or administrative law and courts as in France, or open government and investigation by an Ombudsman as in Sweden, or direct democracy as in Switzerland. We had little more than the doctrine of ministerial responsibility and exiguous remedies evolved by the common law. The providential State managed affairs in much the same way as a medieval monarch managed his household.

However, public pressure during the past twenty years or so has led to the creation of a plethora of bodies to control the Administration. We now have scores of tribunals (with a Council to supervise them), a number of Ombudsmen, procedures to investigate complaints against the police, and a host of agencies, commissions, committees, offices and councils, all designed to protect the citizen against arbitrary action and to ensure that his rights are not sacrificed to the convenience of those in authority. The House of Commons is also aiming to strengthen its control by a revised committee system.

All this is well known. It must, however, constantly be borne in mind because the question arises whether we need, in addition, a Bill of Rights. One may, I think, assume that our existing patchwork (or at least the greater part of it) will continue to exist. On the other hand, we need not assume that it has reached its final form. It will no doubt be gradually improved by the same pressure that brought it into being, namely, that of informed public opinion. I stress the word 'informed' because in this whole area knowledge of fact is as important as abstract principle. Take, for example, the question of complaints against the police, which seem to worry many people. In one English county (Kent)

alone in 1979 it cost more than £60,000 to investigate 620
complaints against the police made by 360 people. Of the 620
complaints, 347 were withdrawn or not proceeded with by the
complainant, 260 were not substantiated, and 13 were substantiated (*The Times*, 9 April 1980).

What, then, might be gained by adding to our existing
patchwork another layer of rights and remedies that will require
more officials and more public money? The power of Parliament
would be limited: the courts would be able to invalidate statutes.
The courts would also have wider powers to control Executive
action and to review the merits of administrative decisions. The
power of trades unions might be curbed: at the moment they seem
free to inflict untold damage on innocent persons who have no
means of redress. These advantages, and their extent, would
depend upon the content of a Bill of Rights.

I turn therefore to the second question – which rights should be
included in any Bill of Rights? A prescription of rights embodies
political values and is likely to give rise to controversy. Rights
may be put in three categories. (a) Liberal, for example life,
liberty, security. (b) Democratic, for example the right to vote.
(c) 'Social' and 'economic', including rights to divorce, abortion,
education, work or maintenance, and a minimum income. Most
rights in the European Convention on Human Rights fall into the
first two categories. It appears to me that these are already pretty
well protected in Britain, not only by law, but by our history and
political culture. There seems no urgent need for the enactment
of this particular content, though for the same reason there may
be no strong opposition to it. (There are one or two possible
exceptions, notably the prohibition in Article 3 of the Convention
against 'inhuman or degrading treatment or punishment', which I
discuss below.) But the Convention alone would probably not
satisfy many who want to strengthen rights in the United
Kingdom.

On one side are those who wish to limit the power of
Parliament and of trades unions and to subject the Administration
to closer control by the courts. Statutory enactment of the
Convention would not restrict parliamentary power, not only
because (as it is claimed) one Parliament cannot bind its
successors, but also because a number of Articles, in effect,
permit rights to be restricted 'in accordance with the law'. Nor

would such a statute control trades unions. The Convention protects freedom to join trades unions but (unlike the Universal Declaration of Human Rights in the United Nations) does *not* say that no one may be compelled to join an association. (Judges determined to do justice though the heavens fall might, of course, hold that the 'closed shop' infringes the basic Convention rights to freedom of conscience, speech and association.) On the other side are those who wish to strengthen social and economic rights. The European Convention guarantees the right to marry, but not to divorce, still less to abortion, contraception, etc., which many women feel deeply about. Equally, the Convention is silent about those economic rights contained in the Universal Declaration: 'the right to work, to free choice of employment, to just and favourable conditions of work', 'the right to a standard of living adequate for the health and well-being of himself and of his family, including food, clothing, housing and medical care and necessary social services', and so on. To some people it may seem self-evident that the collectivist State ought to be hamstrung by law; to others, that beneficent government should be nourished and fortified. On what grounds ought one set of values to prevail by means of rules interpreted and applied by the courts rather than by the democratic process? One can foresee a rough passage for a new Bill of Rights in Britain.

How broadly or narrowly should rights be defined? It has been said that the only absolute right is the right to equal consideration. That is procedural. Statements of substantive rights need to be qualified, and to be interpreted when actual cases are decided, in order to protect other values, notably the rights of other persons. One possibility, as in India, is to draft a document at length and in detail. That would introduce rigidity and probably necessitate fairly frequent amendment. Another possibility, as in the United States, is to use very general terms, leaving the courts to qualify and interpret them. Take, for example, the unqualified prescription in the European Convention that 'no one shall be subjected to torture or to inhuman or degrading treatment or punishment' (Article 3). Is birching in the Isle of Man (which was held to contravene this) inhuman and degrading? Is it more so than capital punishment or life imprisonment or incarceration in a maximum security prison? Others wiser than I may be able to find confident answers by intuition or natural law or some utilitarian calculus; but their confidence will not necessarily be generally shared, and may indeed affront the will of a majority expressed through a democratically elected legislature. As I noted above, the ideals of liberalism and democracy may conflict. Conflict is likely to be more acute when majorities are large or interests are strong or policy questions are involved. In such circumstances, judges are drawn into the arena of politics.

The final question is what changes in institutions and attitudes would be involved if a Bill of Rights were introduced? It is reasonably clear that, depending on the *content* of a Bill of Rights, changes – more or less profound – would be required in the United Kingdom. I mention three of these.

1 *Parliament*. To be effective, rights should be entrenched. Parliamentary supremacy would have to be either abolished or modified by rules prescribing special procedures or enhanced majorities for amendments to a Bill of Rights. How could this be done? The question has engendered a lively debate and I shall not attempt to add to it, except to note that special procedures would probably be needed for dealing with legislation that might appear, directly or indirectly, to affect entrenched rights.

2 *The Courts*. As I indicated earlier, the courts would tend to become politicised. Judges might be called upon to invalidate a statute to the extent that it interfered with the exercise of a right; or to decide whether legislation is of a sort that requires a special parliamentary procedure or majority; or to substitute their discretion for that of Ministers, officials or other public authorities. Some of the consequences can be envisaged: strife between Parliament and the courts; public criticism of judges instead of (or as well as) politicians and administrators; and political appointments to the Bench as it became less distinguishable from the legislature. All this is illustrated in the history of the Supreme Court of the United States.

3 *Attitudes*. Lord Devlin once observed that the British have no more wish to be governed by judges than they have to be judged by administrators (*The Times*, 27 October 1976). If we are to be governed by judges, we shall need rather more public respect for legality than we have had in recent years. By repect for legality I mean respect for rules simply because they are made by a legitimate authority. But British governments have learned to their cost that it is one thing to make rules and another to get

them obeyed. Industrial relations legislation is perhaps the best illustration of this. Consider the fate of the Industrial Relations Act 1971. If statutes cannot control trades unions, what reason is there to expect that a Bill of Rights and judicial decisions will do so? On the other hand, if trades unions are to be largely free to do as they please, why should less powerful interests be subject to judicial restraint? It may be expedient to control the weak and not the strong, but that sort of expediency makes a mockery of the ideal of enforceable and universal rights.

Conclusion

I doubt whether a United Kingdom Bill of Rights incorporating only the rights in the European Convention would enhance our rights and freedoms to any substantial extent. It would, however, entail profound changes in Parliament and the courts and probably mean some increase in bureaucracy and public expenditure. A more comprehensive Bill of Rights, containing some social and economic guarantees and restraints on trade union power would be unlikely to succeed.

I do not argue that all is well in the United Kingdom. The manifold ills that afflict us may, however, be better treated by other prescriptions. Proportional representation would strengthen moderate opinion and weaken trades unions' influence in the House of Commons. Cuts in public services, together with some redistribution of income, would allow individuals a greater measure of free choice in the market place. The Council on Tribunals could be strengthened – it has recently called for wider powers. Administrative discretion in local offices could be reduced by more detailed and uniform regulations. Better ways could be found to inform citizens about rights and remedies. More open government at all levels would make it easier to uncover irregularity and injustice. These are only a few items taken from the extensive catalogue of ideas compiled by reformers in recent years.

One last point. I have not mentioned the anomaly that persons in the United Kingdom may seek remedies under the European Convention on Human Rights in Strasbourg but not in domestic courts. Nor have I mentioned the implications for human rights of judgments by the European Court of Justice. It may be argued that the European Convention ought to be enacted as part of

United Kingdom law, on the rather narrow ground that this
would be the only way to end an anomaly. It would, I think, be
regrettable if those who are concerned about human rights in
Britain were content to stop there.

INTRODUCING A BILL OF RIGHTS

Lord Wade

For some years there has been a growing interest in the United Kingdom in the concept of a Bill of Rights. This marks a movement away from the traditional view, on which most lawyers in Britain have been brought up, namely that civil liberties can adequately be protected by the development of the common law, case by case, or by the introduction by Parliament of a diversity of specific remedies to rectify particular ills. A gradual change in attitude to this subject has been taking place. Distinguished lawyers, of whom Lord Scarman is a notable example, have come out in favour of a statement of general principle on the lines of a Bill of Rights. He gave powerful support to the Bill I introduced in the House of Lords.

There are several strands of thought which have influenced opinion in favour of this reform. In the first place, it is recognised that, today, the activities of Parliament and the Executive affect to such an increasing extent every aspect of our social life, and society is so complex, that there is greater need for some additional protection of individual human rights. Second, while changes in the law should still be the responsibility of Parliament, greater respect for the principles of Equity should be permissible in the interpretation of the law. To this must be added the contention that, so far as basic liberties and human rights are concerned, these can no longer be regarded as matters of purely domestic or national relevance. The whole subject has become international in character. Furthermore, the United Kingdom is already committed to the European Convention together with some of its Protocols. The most practical step forward is, therefore, to incorporate the terms of the Convention into our domestic law. The problem has now become not just whether there should be a Bill of Rights but rather what form it should take.

During the debate in the House of Lords about my own Bill, it appeared that much of the argument against was, in effect, against our ever having signed the Convention rather than against the contents of the Bill itself. Nevertheless, I recognise that there are important points that deserve the most careful consideration.

Some advocates of a Bill of Rights take the view that the best course would be to draw up a completely new set of principles, which would be more up-to-date than the wording of the European Convention. The objections to this are, in my view, twofold: (a) The existence of two sets of principles alongside each other would create confusion and would certainly cause difficulties if the principles had to be interpreted by the courts; (b) the practical obstacles that would arise in getting a new agreed set of principles approved by Parliament would be considerable. One can foresee the time that would be taken up in obtaining agreement in Parliament on each separate Article, and doubtless many amendments having to be debated and voted on. Although there is undoubtedly a case for a revised wording, the long delay involved suggests that it would be advisable to rely on the principles of the European Convention to which the United Kingdom is already committed. It is for this reason that much of the argument over a Bill of Rights has turned on the advantages or disadvantages of incorporation of the Articles of the Convention into our domestic law. This is not a matter of mere academic interest.

Most member countries of the European Convention have in one form or another incorporated the terms of the Convention into their domestic law. The United Kingdom is an exception. By signing the Convention and ratifying certain of the Protocols, we are in the position of having signed and ratified a Treaty, but under our constitution this gives no right of action in our domestic courts. By Article 1 the United Kingdom has undertaken to secure for everyone within its jurisdiction the rights and freedoms set out in the Convention, but the Government is not only under a Treaty obligation to other member states; it is under some moral obligation to its own citizens. Yet under our constitution this gives no right of action to individual citizens against their own government for breaches of the Convention. Their only remedy is to bring a case to the European Commission and ultimately to the European Court of Human Rights. The issue now before the British Parliament is whether individual citizens should have the right to go to a British court. This proposal would still leave the Treaty obligations intact, though it would in all probability reduce the number of cases that might come before the Commission. The discussions about this controversial issue have highlighted a number of points of constitutional importance and reference must be made to two in particular – these relate to *Derogation* and *Entrenchment.*

Article 15 of the European Convention provides that a member nation(a High Contracting Party) may 'in time of war or other public emergency threatening the life of the nation' take measures derogating from its obligations, but strict limits are imposed in the clauses of Article 15 as to permissible grounds and the procedures to be followed. It is well enough known that questions arising from Article 15 have been considered by the European Commission. The incorporation of the terms of the Convention would *not* affect the responsibilities of the United Kingdom under its Treaty obligations, but it *would* introduce a new factor. In drawing attention to this I am not departing from my view that incorporation should take place. When I introduced my Bill it seemed, at first sight, that the position would be adequately covered by incorporation of Article 15, but on reflection and in the light of comments by the House of Lords Select Committee[1], I came to the conclusion that in the event of an outbreak of war or other public emergency it would be permissible for an individual citizen to question in court whether in fact a state of war or other public emergency did exist. If this course were followed it might delay the introduction of the powers contained in Article 15 in a way that might make them ineffective. To meet this possible situation I introduced Clause 4 on derogation into my Bill. Spokesmen from both Government and Opposition Front Benches in the Lords approved this Clause, but it still remains to be seen whether it will be accepted in the Commons.

Constitutionally the most fundamental issue that either my Bill or any other Bill of Rights raises is the question as to whether any Parliament should be placed in a position of being able to bind its successors. In other words should there be any form of entrenchment? This was discussed at considerable length by the House of Lords Select Committee. Could or should some exceptional weight be given to the observance of the principles of the European Convention without introducing some degree of entrenchment into our constitution? My attempt to deal with this is to be found in Clause 3 of my Bill.

Clause 3, in effect, provides that new enactments would be interpreted by the courts on the assumption that Parliament intended that the principles of the Convention should be complied with in future legislation, unless it *expressly* indicated the contrary or could not be interpreted in any other way than as conflicting with an Article of the Convention. Parliament (that is the then existing Parliament) would remain sovereign. The courts would be bound to carry out the wishes of Parliament. But there is a political significance in dealing in this way with the undoubted dilemma, which constitutional lawyers have raised. Parliament would have the power to contravene its Treaty obligations, but any Government sensitive to public opinion would feel some hesitation in openly committing a breach of Treaty and, apart from public opinion, it would have to face the consequences of such a breach. In practice this provision, as outlined in Clause 3 of my Bill, might well prove effective, perhaps almost as effective as an entrenched clause in our constitution. In any event, in view of the hazards involved in amending the constitution, I believe my proposal to be the best way ahead. Others can continue to debate the merits and demerits of introducing a Bill of Rights. My proposal is that we should have a Bill of Rights and the precise form and mechanisms are contained in the Bill which is set out below.

A
BILL
(as amended on Report)
intituled
An Act to render the provisions of the European   A.D. 1979
Convention for the Protection of Human Rights
enforceable in the courts of the United Kingdom.

Be it enacted by the Queen's most Excellent
Majesty, by and with the advice and consent of
the Lords Spiritual and Temporal, and Commons,
in this present Parliament assembled, and by

the authority of the same, as follows:-

1 The Convention for the Protection of Human Rights and Fundamental Freedoms signed by Governments being Members of the Council of Europe at Rome on 4th November 1950, together with such Protocols thereto as shall have been ratified by the Government of the United Kingdom, shall subject to any reservations thereto by the Government of the United Kingdom immediately upon the passing of this Act have the force of law, and shall be enforceable by action in the Courts of the United Kingdom.

Convention to be enforceable in courts.

2 In case of conflict between any laws or enactments prior to the passing of this Act and the provisions of the said Convention and such Protocols as shall have been ratified by the Government of the United Kingdom and subject to any reservations thereto, the said Convention and Protocols shall prevail.

Convention to prevail over previous enactments.

3 In case of conflict between any enactment subsequent to the passing of this Act and the provisions of the said Convention and such Protocols as shall have been ratified by the Government of the United Kingdom and subject to any reservations thereto, such enactment passed after the passing of this Act shall be deemed to be subject to the provisions of the said Convention and Protocols and shall be so construed unless such subsequent enactment provides otherwise or does not admit of any construction compatible with the provisions of this Act.

Convention to prevail over subsequent enactments unless stated to the contrary.

4 (1) Notwithstanding anything contained in section 1 of this Act and subject to subsections (2) and (3) of this section, in time of war or other public emergency threatening the life of the nation Her Majesty by Order in Council may take measures derogating from the obligations of the Government of the United Kingdom

Derogating measures.

under the said Convention and Protocols
('derogating measures').

(2) No derogation from Articles 2 (except
in respect of deaths resulting from lawful acts of
war), 3, 4 (paragraph 1) and 7 of the said
Convention shall be made under the provisions
of this section.

(3) No derogating measures shall have any
effect on the obligations of the Government of
the United Kingdom under international law.

(4) For the purposes of this Act, a declaration
by Her Majesty by Order in Council that there
exists for the purposes of any derogating
measures a time of war or other emergency
threatening the life of the nation shall be conclusive.

5 For the purposes of this Act –   Definitions

'Convention' means Articles 1 to 18 inclusive and Article 60 of the said Convention;

'Protocols' means Articles 1 to 3 inclusive
of the (First) Protocol to the said Convention;

'reservations' means the Reservation made
to the (First) Protocol (Article 2) by the United
Kingdom under Article 64 of the said Convention.

6 (1) This Act may be cited as the Bill of   Short title
Rights Act 1979.   and extent.

(2) This Act extends to Northern Ireland.

ARGUMENTS AGAINST A BILL OF RIGHTS

Lord Boston of Faversham

Before coming to the substance of my argument against the proposal to introduce a Bill of Rights three preliminary points should be made. The first is that the Standing Advisory Commission on Human Rights in Northern Ireland have performed an immensely valuable service in stimulating the current debate about the protection of human rights by law. Whatever the outcome, whatever view one takes of the specific matters discussed, the debate is an important one – and it is important that it should take place. Let us never overlook the fact that (though we may wish to make improvements in our own country) there are still, sadly, many parts of the world where even a *debate* of this kind could not take place, let alone where rights of the kind which we take for granted could be introduced.

The next point is simply this – none of us, whether we are in favour of a Bill of Rights or whether we are against it, has (or has claimed) a monopoly of enthusiasm for promoting human rights. Equally nobody on the one side will say of anybody on the other side that he or she is wanting, when it comes to furthering those aims. Indeed, this is something which emerged during the discussions in the House of Lords Select Committee on a Bill of Rights (on Lord Wade's Bill). The sentiment is enshrined in a passage in the Report of the Select Committee which says:

> The Committee feels it is of great importance to emphasise that, although some of the members favour incorporation of the (European) Convention into United Kingdom law and some oppose it, there was unanimity of view on the need to protect and advance human rights and unanimous recognition that both sides were wholly committed to the promotion of human rights.[1]

It is worth placing this on the record so that no-one will claim that those of us who do not happen to favour Lord Wade's Bill, nor incorporation of the European Convention on Human Rights, do not care enough about human rights.

My final prefatory point is perhaps the converse of the

previous one. It is that, while there may be room for improvement, the record of the United Kingdom on human rights is a good one – indeed it is exemplary. (Thus just as one misconception might suggest those opposed to a Bill of Rights are insufficiently concerned with the protection of human rights, the converse misconception would have it that those who support a Bill are, by that token, condemning their own country.) Those of us who have served, for instance, at the United Nations have found it of immense value to refer to this country's record – and to the reforms and safeguards introduced over the years, including recent examples in tackling discrimination through such bodies as the Commission for Racial Equality and the Equal Opportunities Commission. It is of tremendous value, in the United Nations General Assembly's Third Committee which deals with human rights matters, to be able to say what has been and is *being* done in the United Kingdom when trying to encourage other countries to further the cause of human rights. We tend to be the first to criticise ourselves – and that, no doubt, is good. But we should not shrink from acknowledging that we have also set high standards through *example*.

As I am sure has now been deduced I was amongst those members of the Select Committee of the House of Lords who voted against incorporating the European Convention on Human Rights into our law. I want to go through some of the arguments that led to that view and, in doing so, think it important to note that the arguments for and against a Bill of Rights cut right across party political lines. There are people in all the main parties in Parliament who support and oppose incorporation. It is, indeed, not without significance that this feature also applies to the Cross-Benchers in the House of Lords, including the Law Lords who are divided amongst themselves. In what I shall say, in talking of a Bill of Rights, my point of reference will be the proposals made, particularly in Lord Wade's Bill, that there should be incorporation of the European Convention on Human Rights.

One of the most fundamental objections to incorporation of the Convention is that it would – as the House of Lords Select Committee observed in stating the arguments against incorporation – graft onto the existing law, an Act of Parliament which would be in a form totally at variance with any existing legislation and in a way which would be incompatible with such legislation. It has long been accepted under our constitution that Parliament legislates in a specific form, and that the role of the courts is to *interpret* that legislation. If we took the course proposed by those who wish to incorporate the Convention, we would be opening up a wide variety of legislative policies in a very general way and handing them over to the judiciary for detailed *development* (not just interpretation) on such subjects as, say, race relations, freedom of speech, freedom of the Press, privacy, education, and forms of punishment. Yet those are matters which, under our constitution, have been the province of the legislature. Moreover, although it is perhaps of minor significance there is an additional dimension which I do not believe has been explored sufficiently. It is that certain aspects of statute law – of law and order legislation for instance relating to public order and marches – allow scope for *local* needs and inclinations and adaptation through local, private Acts of Parliament.[2] The implications so far as scope for local variations and choice are concerned have not been considered in discussions about a Bill of Rights. It could well be that the courts would find themselves drawn into attempting different interpretations and *different developments* of the law for different parts of the country.

I share the view of those who say that under a Bill of Rights it would not be the case that the role of the courts would remain similar to the role they have always had at common law. For at common law the development of legal principles has been a slow process – evolving from case to case. Under a Bill of Rights incorporating the European Convention, however, the courts would start off with a set of broad principles and would then have a free hand to decide how to apply those principles to the individual cases that came before them.

It has been suggested by at least one supporter of a Bill of Rights that those of us who are against a Bill, are really saying our judges are not capable of taking on the tasks which would be involved if the Convention was incorporated. Of course, we are saying nothing of the kind – and it would be absurd to do so. The accomplishments of our courts are unsurpassed anywhere in the world, and they are perfectly capable of undertaking any tasks Parliament gives them. What we *do* say is that the role thus granted to judges is not one they should have to fulfil. Some tasks

should remain with Parliament alone. Indeed leading members
of the judiciary have argued against the change that would be
involved. As the late Lord Morris of Borth-y-Gest said in a
debate on the Bill of Rights:

> Before we put a measure on the Statute Book must we not be
> quite certain that there is a need and that a need has been
> proved to legislate in the proposed terms? Very often legislation
> comes about as a result of some strong demands, often
> vigorously expressed. We have not, I think, experienced such
> processes. However, my opposition to the suggested legislation
> does not rest on my view that no substantial advantage has
> been shown to result from the passing of the Bill, but rather on
> my view that there would be positive and serious disadvantages.
> The legislation would be in a form quite different from the
> accepted style of legislation in this country. It would always be
> possible to change our scheme of things; it would always be
> possible to legislate and to lay down some precept or good
> intention and then to say, 'Now we leave it to the judges to
> work it out'. I should be wholly opposed to any such system. In
> my view, it would be quite undesirable for Parliament partly to
> legislate and then to hand over the matter to the judges and
> require them to legislate as to the remainder. I am quite sure
> that Her Majesty's judges will do whatever they are asked to
> do by Parliament. But, I am also sure that they would not ask
> to have powers put upon them to make decisions which really
> are decisions as to the content of legislation.[3]

Another of the Law Lords, Lord Diplock, spoke out against the
Bill, and against incorporation:

> It is inevitable in a modern society, in which judges have to
> interpret social legislation about which strong political views
> are held on either side, that this tends to bring judges into the
> political arena . . . If we are to pass a Bill of Rights in the form
> of the European Convention, it is inevitable that that tendency
> will increase, because a Bill of Rights in that form compels the
> Judiciary to make political decisions.[4]

Lord Diplock went on to point out that during the debate on the
Bill of Rights and the Convention, stress had been laid on the first
sentence of each of the Convention's Articles cast in absolute

terms: everyone shall have a right to privacy, everyone shall have a right to freedom of expression, or whatever it may be. But little attention had been attached to the small print, to the second sentence, providing conditions in which derogation can be made from those rights which are so absolutely expressed in the first sentence. He mentioned that there was some judicial experience in this country of interpreting Bills of Rights, since the Judicial Committee of the Privy Council deals with appeals from a number of independent Commonwealth countries who have entrenched in their constitutions, Bills of Rights in terms often similar to those in the European Convention. He thus spoke with experience of interpreting and applying entrenched provisions for human rights and he said:

> No human right can be absolute. Even the right to life – 'thou shalt not kill' – is, in the Convention, subject to exceptions which are spelled out specifically. Those present no difficulties. But when you come to the other rights – the right to privacy in Article 8, the right to freedom of thought and conscience in Article 9, the right to freedom of expression in Article 10 and the right to freedom of association in Article 11 – these are subject to an exception permitting derogation from the absolute right. I shall take the exception from Article 8 on privacy, which is . . . subject to such exception as is necessary, 'In a democratic society in the interests of national security, public safety or the economic well-being of the country, for the prevention of disorder or crime, for the protection of health or morals, or for the protection of the rights and freedoms of others.' That, with slight variations, runs like a refrain through those rights . . .

Lord Diplock then drew attention to the additional exception which is inevitable with a Bill of Rights of this kind – the exception for a public emergency threatening the life of the nation. Again, derogation from the rights is permitted 'to the extent strictly required by the exigencies of the situation'. He dealt first with the *emergency* exception because it was simpler (the current example is of course Northern Ireland), and he used these words:

> It lies upon judges to decide whether a derogation satisfies the

requirement of being strictly required by the exigencies of the situation. First, let me say that judges, by their training, by their experience, by the comparative isolation in which, by reason of their office, they are bound to live, are ill-fitted, compared with commoners, to decide in an emergency what the exigencies of a situation require. Secondly, it has to be decided by judges applying the judicial process, and the judicial process requires judges to act on evidence and not upon their own notions.

In emergencies, Governments act upon intelligence, which very often cannot be disclosed and put in evidence at all, so as to preserve the secrecy of sources, or, it may be, in order to avoid exacerbating the situation. Is it right that in an emergency the decision as to what is necessary to deal with the exigencies of the situation should be left to me rather than to Government? Power hungry as I may be, I would hesitate to regard myself as fit to make that decision.[5]

Lord Diplock considered ordinary human rights, where there was no question of an emergency, but where someone challenges a previous Act of Parliament and claims it diminishes the absolute right enshrined in an Article of the Convention. Here, it has to be decided whether the derogation from the right is one which, in a democratic society, is necessary for the protection of public health, safety, economic well-being, or the like. Such decisions depend on the social and political philosophy one holds dear, and, as Lord Diplock, said:

In a democratic society – those are the words in the Convention – it seems to me, power hungry as I am, that those who represent the people and have been elected democratically in a representative Parliament know better and are better judges of that than appointed judges, who have been appointed not for their social philosophies or their politics but because of their qualification in the law. If this Bill becomes law in its present form, it will be open to every fanatic, every crackpot, to challenge any law they disagree with and which they think – indeed can verily suggest – detracts little or anything at all from the absolute right conferred by the first sentence in each Article. . . . The administration of justice in our country depends upon the respect which all people of all political views feel for the judges, and in my opinion that respect depends very much upon keeping judges out of politics. To pass this Bill of Rights cannot but have the tendency to bring judges more and more into politics. That seems to me to be a sufficient disadvantage, and so far as I am concerned, when it is put into the balance, it tips it down upon the side of not passing a Bill in the form of that which is proposed.

As a former Law Lord, Lord Devlin, wrote not long ago: the British have no more wish to be governed by judges than they have to be judged by administrators. Taken together then these are powerful and experienced judicial voices which endorse this major argument against incorporation of the European Convention on Human Rights.

As the Select Committee of the House of Lords pointed out, Parliament has repeatedly demonstrated that it is ready to move into new areas of law-making where the need to meet fresh social problems has been shown. It is far better for Parliament to enact detailed legislation on such matters as sex discrimination and race relations, than to leave it to unelected judges to develop policies and work out how they should be applied. (Of course, a legislative role is given to some of Her Majesty's judges in the House of Lords – the Law Lords – where part of their function is to play a full and immensely valuable part in the statute law-making process. But it is in *that* way that they are meant to fulfil that particular part of their function – and that is quite separate and distinct from their judicial role.)

Another matter of great concern is the *uncertainty* in the law which those of us who are against a Bill of Rights foresee arising – something already touched on in the quoted views of Lord Diplock. I am sure we would all agree that, so far as possible, the law should be clear and certain. To achieve as much is one of the principal roles of those of us who are legislators. But if the European Convention which is couched in broad terms proclaiming wide generalisations open to a variety of interpretations were made part of our domestic law, it would introduce a vast area of uncertainty into our law. It would become much more difficult for individual people as well as companies and other bodies to get confident advice about their rights and obligations, their powers and their liabilities. As the House of Lords Select

Committee's Report put it:

> The uncertainty thus brought into our law would itself afford
> opportunity for exploiting endless challenges in the courts or
> before any tribunal to the validity of the existing laws. No one
> would know where he stood until each question had been
> tested afresh, and the least that can be said is that there is the
> prospects of a very great extension of litigation in the courts.[6]

. The vague, general and uncertain terms of the Convention
have been noted by many people. Lord Morris of Borth-y-Gest
drew attention to Article 8, the first part of which says that
'Everyone has the right to respect for his private and family life,
his home and his correspondence'. He pointed out that Parliament
has had many debates about the introduction of appropriate
legislation to prevent unjustifiable invasions of privacy. As Lord
Morris said, there are intractable problems – how do we do it? To
use Lord Morris's own words:

> Are we now to put on the Statute Book that 'Everyone has the
> right to respect for his private and family life, his home and his
> correspondence' subject always to the second part, and leave
> it to the courts – at the instance of any number of ingenious
> people who could raise all sorts of proceedings – to say what
> this means? Is Parliament to say, 'We abrogate; we have been
> thinking about how to deal with invasions of privacy. We have
> failed to find any methods. We abandon it all. We say that we
> will pass the Bill with the words, 'Everyone has the right to
> respect for his private and family life, his home and his
> correspondence, subject only of course to the second paragraph'
> to which the learned and noble Lord Diplock referred. . . .
> Your Lordships take an infinity of trouble when a Bill is
> introduced here to ensure that the wording is right. Sometimes
> it takes many days or weeks to consider all the possibilities of
> wording. Who could decide what that Article means? I am
> merely putting forward illustrations. In any view, the enacted
> law ought to be clear and certain. To enact this Bill would
> involve and introduce a parade of uncertainties. I hope that
> your Lordships will not pass the Bill.[7]

Anxiety about uncertainty has been expressed too by Lord
Foot. As he said, these worries are not just theoretical objections

to introducing theoretical uncertainties into our legal system – they are much more specific. They amount to fear that we would introduce uncertainty as to what are the human rights in this country. It is a commonplace that in this country the way we have defined individual rights in the past has not been through generalised solemn pronouncements about the virtues of freedom of expression and of speech and so on. The way we have proceeded under our constitution is by seeking to establish remedies available to the individual if his civil rights are in fact infringed, so that he can go to a court to obtain that remedy. The great virtue is that the citizen can be reasonably certain of (and can reasonably ascertain) his rights. The danger in importing the Convention into our law is that it will gratuitously introduce a new element of uncertainty.

It is also noteworthy in this regard that the Law Society came out strongly against the proposed Bill both in evidence to the Select Committee of the House of Lords and in a note by its Law Reform Committee published subsequently. Amongst the Law Society's strongest objections to incorporating the European Convention, was the problem of the uncertainties that would arise in our law.

It has already been widely acknowledged by leading authorities on both sides of the argument, that incorporation would lead to a sizeable increase in litigation. Of course, this would be splendid for the lawyers and a bonanza for the Bar. But as a practising member of the Bar I find myself, not for the first time, concerned to advocate policies against more work and income for my profession!

Before turning to other arguments against a Bill of Rights and incorporation, I would just mention one other point in connection with the law of privacy used in illustration by Lord Morris of Borth-y-Gest. This is an example of an area which Parliament has considered but either failed or decided not to legislate on. It is at least arguable that in such circumstances it would be quite wrong for the judges to attempt to 'legislate' or develop the law on such a matter at all. Certainly it raises a number of questions which need to be answered. It is one thing for Parliament to legislate in detail on something, thus imposing obligations or conferring rights, or for Parliament simply not to consider legislating on a particular matter. It is another thing for Parlia-

ment to decide *not* to legislate in detail. Does that leave the door
open to providing remedies by other means – through, for
example, the judges? Or would that be wrong? If not wrong,
would it perhaps be undesirable – or likely to bring the courts into
the political arena, and indeed into a clash with Parliament?
Would that be better avoided? Should the judges refrain from
intervening in an area where Parliament has itself decided *not* to
go? I mention such points only in passing but they may deserve
further thought.

One matter which was clarified by the Report of the Select
Committee was that it was common ground that human rights are
not better protected in other countries which do have a code of
fundamental human rights. On the contrary, we received much
well informed evidence to the effect that we, in this country, are
far in advance of the European Convention. Thus Mr Cedric
Thornberry, Governor of the British Institute of Human Rights,
went so far as to say that the incorporation of the Convention into
the fabric of our society 'would retard rather than advance the
cause of human rights in Britain'.[8]

A further clarification concerned what are alleged to be
existing defects in our law. Of course, our law is far from perfect,
and there is no cause for complacency. But it emerged that the
existing defects which the Convention might 'put right' were
relatively trifling and marginal matters which were readily
capable of reform already, generally by administrative, but
certainly by legislative, means. Nor is it the case that under the
Convention relatively more cases are brought against this
country than against other comparable countries. On the contrary,
the figures show that, if anything, the claims against Germany
have been more than against ourselves – though Germany has
the full panoply of Bill of Rights legislation. Not only do they
have the European Convention in their law; they have their
elaborate 'basic law', which sets out in a much more detailed
form than the Convention itself all kinds of fundamental rights.
Yet there are as many cases in relation to Germany as to
ourselves. Lord Diplock in commenting on the position in
Germany where the Constitution entrenches provisions similar
to the Bill of Rights we are considering noted:

Since 1952, 40,000 cases have been brought in the constitutional courts. About five of those cases were really important, but every one of them had to be dealt with. At the rate of something like 1,700 cases a year, that is two or three times the total case load of the Civil Division of the Court of Appeal in this country.[9]

Similarly, the then Lord Chancellor, Lord Elwyn-Jones, endorsed the point made by the Select Committee that there is no lack of criticism of the Convention itself. Even twenty-eight years ago when it was drawn up it represented only the minimum standards accepted by the participating countries, and he agreed with the Committee that there was no doubt that in a good many respects our present law can claim to do a good deal better than the minimum standards laid down in the Convention. He too had come to the conclusion (contrary to the impression conveyed by some people) that our record in being brought before the European Commission and the Court was no worse than those of other countries – including those which had incorporated the Convention into their domestic law. He quoted figures:

In 1975 and 1976, about 750 individual applications were registered out of around 4,000 communications to the Commission. Out of the 13 Convention countries which recognize the right of individual petition, we lie second in the league table to the Federal Republic of Germany, from which there were 231 applications, while there were 205 from ourselves. France . . . has not accepted the right of individual petition at all. If one looks at the ratio of the number of applications made per million of population of each country, the picture . . . is as follows. I do not know how valuable these statistics are, but they are interesting *en passant*. The league table is headed by Switzerland, with 9.5 applications per million of the population . . . followed by Austria, 8; Belgium, 7; West Germany, 3.8; ourselves, 3.6; . . . Denmark, 3.5. So . . . those figures do not support the argument that our record is worse than that of other countries, or that we are politically vulnerable because of nonincorporation.[10]

These considerations are summed up in passages from the Report of the Select Committee:

The present situation in the United Kingdom is in accord with the original philosophy of the European Convention. The Convention was intended to lay down minimum standards of human rights which it was assumed would be in accord with the spirit of all the legal systems of the signatories to the Convention. It was always contemplated, as in fact has proved to be the case, that from time to time there would be conflicts between the domestic laws of the signatory states and the Convention, and for this reason the Convention set up machinery by way of the European Commission and the European Court to deal with such cases. Such conflicts have inevitably arisen in all signatory states, whether or not the Convention is part of their domestic law. It is in accordance with the spirit of the Convention that, when it emerges that there is such a conflict in the case of the United Kingdom, this should be put right. Where necessary this can be done by legislation, but often the deficiency will call for no more than a change of administrative regulation or instructions. But it is no more unflattering to this country than it is to any other signatory of the Convention if the kind of dispute contemplated by the drafters of the Convention from time to time goes to Strasbourg for argument; and it is not the case, as some of the witnesses assumed, that relatively more cases have gone to the Commission from the United Kingdom than from other countries. Even on the most unfavourable view of the extent to which United Kingdom law at present falls short of the standards of the Convention, there are no more than a few marginal situations where the incorporation of a Bill of Rights might bestow a remedy where present law does not do so.[11]

And I should add to this that there is no reason to suppose the Government and Parliament are likely to proceed in ignorance of the country's international commitments in the absence of incorporation. Indeed the Select Committee had examples before it of proposals which had been modified by Government at the stage of preliminary consideration precisely to take account of the Convention. Of course it is always hazardous to be too dogmatic. If it *were* to be the case that Parliament, on the invitation of the Government of the day, enacted measures which were at variance with our international obligations under the Convention, then we might indeed need to look again at the situation to see whether *first* a Bill of Rights was, after all, necessary and *second* whether it could put that situation right. In raising this I have in mind the new immigration rules just passed by Parliament. I have no wish to pursue any party point so I shall not discuss the merits of the matter here. But I would note, in as non-partisan a way as I can, that it is at least strongly arguable that the new rules run counter to the requirements of the Convention. If that is shown to be so, and the position is not put right, and perhaps other violations occurred, then, in those circumstances, we might need to ask ourselves the questions I have posed. Even then, I would still need to be persuaded that a Bill of Rights *was* needed and *could* put right those deficiencies.

I return now to the main objections of those of us who oppose a Bill of Rights and the fundamental questions those objections raise. They are, for example, who should be responsible for reforming and developing our laws? Whose responsibility is it to legislate? In whom should power reside? Whose task should it be to intervene in new areas of law reform and who should formulate and introduce new, detailed measures? Should it be Parliament with its representative democratic elements? Or should it be the non-elected judges? I believe that part at least of this argument is about power, where power resides *and should reside* in our democracy and under our constitution. These are matters of the highest constitutional significance.

As I have said, our judges are able people, perfectly capable of doing whatever Parliament asks them to do. But the real question is what Parliament should empower them to do, not a question of what they are capable of doing. The judges are powerful – and rightly so. Their power derives from the statutory authority Parliament provides, from the common law, from their own qualifications and intellectual qualities. It is true that the power they possess through the common law is considerable. To develop the law through interpretation and the gradual process of reform has, indeed, brought immense benefits over the centuries. It is, though, one thing to draw benefits from the gradual developments which have taken place over the centuries, and quite another suddenly to add a significant if not vast new role and purpose. The change would be quite unlike any change that has gone before. Those who are against a Bill of Rights are not saying 'don't let's reform the law'. On the contrary, we say 'let us continue to urge Parliament to bring in the necessary reforms'. What I have said may seem to some to be negative; I hope not, for I believe passionately and *positively* in the case I've been trying to put. Those of us who take this view do not feel in any way *defensive* towards it; nor, still less, do we feel the present system needs to be excused in any way. Although it needs improvement, I would argue *positively* in its favour. But let me conclude with a specific and entirely positive proposal.

Just as I believe the onus is on those who wish to have a Bill of Rights to prove the need, so I also accept that we *all* have an obligation to do all we can to improve the present system – and not take refuge in complacency. I have long been conscious of the need to try to set up some machinery to ensure that reforms in the human rights sphere are actively pursued and that the necessary detailed legislation is introduced. Previously I have only hinted at the concrete steps which should be taken – let me now say how we should set about introducing specific reforms in the human rights sphere.

In the debate on Lord Wade's Bill in the House of Lords, Lord Elwyn-Jones said:

> We must indeed aim to observe and maintain to the full the principles embodied in the Convention; and it may well be that special measures are required for this purpose . . . Twenty-five years have passed since we ratified the Convention. Times have changed, and the interpretation of the Convention and its provisions has developed, not always in every respect on predictable lines. The better course for protecting the citizen's fundamental rights may now well be to carry out a general review of our law to identify any points on which it falls short of the Convention's ideals, and remedy any defects or shortfall in our legal provisions or procedures. . . . The most effective course may be to set up a Standing Commission on Human Rights charged with this specific task. I do not mean by this a Human Rights Commission with the wide functions sometimes suggested for such a body; but there could be advantage in having a Standing Body with the ongoing function of reviewing the law to ensure that it complies with our international obligations on human rights, including the European Convention. I envisage a body, independent of the Government,

with the appropriate range of legal and other expertise, which would make recommendations to the Government; and its reports would be published.[12]

Of course, even with new machinery of some kind, we would still be at the mercy of Parliament, and the parliamentary timetable. But an authoritative body of that kind, coming forward with precise proposals, would be hard to resist (still less, ignore). We have already had practical experience of the way the Law Commission operates and brings forward not only reports on proposals for reform but draft bills as well. It might even be possible to build into the machinery some provision for according legislative priority to its proposals.

So that is one positive proposal. It needs further thought and the details would have to be worked out and spelled out. But it is a start. Whatever our views on the best way forward I am certain we share a passionate devotion to the cause of human rights. Our involvement in the current debate also shows our determination to keep that cause *alive*.

WHAT DOES A BILL OF RIGHTS MEAN IN PRACTICE?

Professor Peter Wallington

In recent years the 'Bill of Rights debate' has really been a debate about whether we should incorporate the European Convention on Human Rights into domestic United Kingdom law, in the manner of Lord Wade's Bill of Rights Bill. It is true that other measures have been canvassed, including patent schemes prepared by various organisations, and there is, as a second runner, the United Nations Covenant on Civil and Political Rights, which the Government has ratified (although here there is no enforcement machinery equivalent to that contained in the European Convention). But for practical purposes the debate concerns whether we should incorporate the Convention, so I shall concentrate on this proposal.

First of all I should state that, on balance, I am a supporter of the Wade approach – although I wish to make detailed criticisms of the terms of the Bill he introduced in the House of Lords. I am not at all sure whether such a measure ought to be described, strictly speaking, as a Bill of Rights. Although the consequences of incorporating the European Convention into United Kingdom law would be complex and far-reaching, the benefits for human rights that would be achieved would in my view be relatively modest. It might be a misleading overstatement to describe such a measure as a Bill of Rights. There is in fact a fundamental paradox about Bills of Rights, in that there is little value in introducing a Bill which serves to accentuate or perpetuate divisions within the community or between communities – whether it be between the trades unions and others over an issue like the 'closed shop', or between the communities in Northern Ireland – but a Bill of Rights that commands united support is unlikely to extend much beyond a platitudinous affirmation of what is already the position.

Be that as it may I shall comment on some of the general and vexed questions raised by proposals to introduce a Bill of Rights into the United Kingdom. In particular I shall deal with the issues raised by the possibilities of entrenchment, the position concerning derogation and what might be called the mechanisms of incorporation. While such matters can appear, in comparison with other considerations relevant to Bills of Rights, rather technical, they nevertheless raise questions of principle.

Entrenchment is an emotive issue – 'giving dead people votes' as it was once graphically described. One of the arguments for at least a limited form of entrenchment of a Bill of Rights is that the United Kingdom is not going to stop being bound by the European Convention on Human Rights, except by positive act of denunciation. It is therefore in the interests of good government that it (government) should be protected, as much as prevented, from accidentally enacting legislation which puts the country in breach of international obligations. It is also a reflection of the importance attached to the protection of basic human rights that they ought not to be subject to the inadvertence of Government Departments. The track record of legislation provides an immediate refutation of any suggestion that Government Departments, or for that matter Parliament, can be trusted always to spot all the implications of legislation that render it inconsistent with the rights of individuals.

Entrenchment against *implied* repeal – requiring Government and Parliament to state specifically that they wish to override recognised and protected rights – is politically controversial only within the circles of pedants. The arguments over whether or not this kind of entrenchment is legally possible seem to me to be quite exceptionally sterile. If, in an important measure enacted after due deliberation, Parliament asks the judges to police its future legislative output for inadvertent infringements of human rights, and not to give effect to them unless told specifically that that is Parliament's wish, it would be a sad reflection on our judges if they were not prepared to do so. I am aware that in saying all this I am not only disagreeing with, but coming close to committing *lèse majesté* against, the distinguished members of the House of Lords Select Committee and their specialist adviser. The Committee concluded that the kind of entrenchment I describe as politically uncontroversial would be legally impossible, and settled instead for a formula of interpretation to protect the Bill from ambiguous implied repeal but not unambiguous implied repeal. I am unrepentant.

In any event, however, I think it may be that there is an

emerging constitutional convention that any major constitutional change – within which category the incorporation of the Convention into domestic law could well be included – should be preceded by a referendum. If that were done, as I believe it ought to be done, prior to the enactment of any Bill of Rights, then judges, to whom we must give credit for a reasonable degree of political sensitivity and awareness, could be expected to accord appropriate deference to the wish of a Parliament supported by the popular will in a referendum, as against the later, often ambiguous and not fully considered will of Parliament – whatever the constitutional experts might say is the law. After all, 'the law' on Parliamentary sovereignty is essentially that to which the judges for the time being give effect. Fortified by the knowledge that the Standing Advisory Commission on Human Rights adopted the view advocated by Jeremy McBride and myself in 1976[1], I can only regret that Lord Wade has, in no offensive sense, shown cowardice in the face of the enemy of pedantic legalism in adopting for his Bill the diluted formula proposed by the Select Committee.

Clause 3 of Lord Wade's Bill provides as follows:

> In case of conflict between any enactment subsequent to the passing of this Act and the provisions of the . . . Convention . . . such enactment . . . shall be deemed to be subject to the provisions of the said Convention . . . and shall be so construed unless such subsequent enactment provides otherwise *or does not admit of any construction compatible with the provisions of this Act.*

It is these last words which were added at the suggestion of the Select Committee, and on which my disagreement is focussed. The practical importance of the disagreement can be illustrated by an example. Recently the Government introduced new immigration controls, which many commentators believe to be sexually and racially discriminatory, and for this reason, to violate the guarantee of family life in Article 8 of the European Convention. The Government, however, says that this is not so, and has not indicated that it wishes to break its international obligations under the Convention. At present the point may be resolved, eventually, at Strasbourg. If Lord Wade's Bill were law without the italicised addition, the Government, being satisfied that it was not violating the Convention, would not include any 'non obstante' clause in the Bill.[2] To the extent that the new rules did violate the Convention, they would be invalid and not enforced by the courts. Thus the Government would be saved the embarrassment of an unintended breach of the Convention, and there would be redress in the courts of the United Kingdom for those affected by the offending provisions of the rules. But with the final words of Clause 3 of Lord Wade's Bill added, the courts could not interfere with the expressed will of Parliament that the law should be as stated, even though, for reasons not appreciated by those concerned in passing the legislation, it was in breach of the Convention and the Bill of Rights.

On either formula, of course, a Government which wished to introduce legislation which it knew might contravene the Convention, regardless of the consequences, and which it could persuade Parliament to agree, could override the terms of the Bill of Rights with legal impunity – at least in our domestic law.

More substantial forms of entrenchment present more difficulty. I do not myself believe that, short of a new constitutional settlement (perhaps embodying a federal solution and with entrenched constitutional provisions of which a Bill of Rights would be but part), there is much value in seeking greater entrenchment against amendment than the protection from implied repeal incorporated in the Canadian Bill of Rights and recommended by the Standing Advisory Commission on Human Rights. Quite apart from the legal difficulties, which are more real in this context, the problem with entrenchment of the kind that requires a particular Parliamentary majority before an amendment can be passed, is that when Parliament determines to turn its face against human rights it generally does so in time of crisis, with support sometimes bordering on the panic-stricken, and by a very large majority. One has only to remember the circumstances of the passage of the Official Secrets Act 1911, or more recently the Prevention of Terrorism legislation, to appreciate that the gravest interferences with individual liberties are likely to be inflicted by a near unanimous Parliament supported by substantial pressure of public opinion. Against this neither a requirement of a special majority in Parliament, nor even a requirement of support in a referendum, are necessarily enough protection. I will leave aside the technical legal arguments about whether any entrenchment of this kind is legally possible. There are certainly difficulties without a new constitutional settlement accompanying the Bill of Rights; equally, if there were a new constitutional settlement with judges reappointed under the provisions of the new Constitution, then the legal revolution would ensure the necessary changes in the principles of Parliamentary sovereignty.

The question of *derogation*, on one aspect of which I have already commented, is difficult. Obviously some freedom must be given to a democratic state to protect the democracy on which other freedoms depend, by curtailing those freedoms in time of emergency. The phenomenon of wartime press censorship is in point. It ought to be equally obvious that it is in time of emergency that the citizen most needs the protection of a Bill of Rights against excessive legislative interference. It is in the nature of Governments to over-react to internal emergencies, and an objective but flexible yardstick to restrain the temptation is of great importance. This is what the European Convention on Human Rights provides. Under Article 15, only such derogation as is necessary – as objectively determined by the European Court, though allowing some margin of discretion to the state authorities – is permitted. And there may be *no* derogation at all in respect of some aspects of the Convention, such as torture. As the Government of the United Kingdom has discovered, excessive responses to an emergency are liable to challenge in the European Court.[3]

The paradox of derogation in relation to entrenchment is that if a Bill of Rights is not entrenched against subsequent express amendment or repeal, no provision is needed for derogation by subsequent statute. If the Bill is entrenched merely against implied repeal, the only value of a procedure for derogation is that a future Government may be spared the embarrassment of a 'non obstante' declaration. Equally, no derogation is permissible in international law which exceeds the terms of Article 15, and it would be inconsistent with a Bill of Rights, one of the purposes of which is to ensure compliance with our international obligations, that derogation should be permitted on less rigorous standards than those required by the Convention itself. Derogation clauses in an unentrenched Bill of Rights seem to me to be largely window-dressing for the benefit of those who do not appreciate this point.

For all of these reasons, the inclusion of a derogation clause (Clause 4) in Lord Wade's Bill seems, with all respect, to be regrettable, as well as technically unnecessary. It is unnecessary because nothing in the rest of the Bill would prevent Parliament from doing what may be done under Clause 4 (or indeed some of the things which specifically may *not* be done under Clause 4). It is regrettable because the measures taken need not meet any justiciable standard of necessity, so that the standards of the Convention are not incorporated into domestic law. Indeed Lord Wade's Bill goes further down the wrong road even than that. It would permit derogation by Order in Council, including – though it is arguable how far the courts would uphold such measures – derogation from existing legally protected rights, such as the suspension of rights to bail or *habeas corpus*. The powers of the executive to curtail individual freedom would on this view actually be *increased* by the Bill – a vivid reminder that lawyers' points can very substantially affect the value of a Bill of Rights, detrimentally as well as favourably. Unless a special saving provision is needed for action under the Emergency Powers Act 1920 (the Canadian Bill of Rights has such a provision for the Canadian equivalent) all derogations from the modest rights safeguarded by the Convention ought at least to be inflicted by statute, with the assent of Parliament. This also applies to derogation in respect of the existing emergency legislation in Northern Ireland.

The last area I wish to cover concerns the *mechanics of incorporation* of the European Convention into UK law – an area which has been largely neglected in the debates so far. It is not surprising, or necessarily undesirable, that it has been neglected. There is a great need for public education on human rights which would not be well served by the debate becoming bogged down in technical details. Despite that, it is on technical points that I wish to concentrate, simply because these points are far more important than has been appreciated by many of the protagonists. The comments I shall make are intended to show why this is so.

The process of incorporation of an international treaty into domestic law is not an altogether simple one, and important consequences can flow from the way in which it is incorporated. At a very basic level, for instance, ought the Convention to be incorporated in the English language only or also in the French? This is not quite such a stupid point as might appear at first hearing; the official texts of the Convention in English and French are equally authoritative, and may well differ in the nuances of interpretation in important respects. For instance, the scope of Article 6 of the Convention, guaranteeing a right to a fair trial in criminal and civil proceedings, applies 'in the determination of his civil rights and obligations'. The scope of this provision in relation to disputes between an individual and a Government Department is unclear, and some assistance has been derived by the European Court itself from comparing the rather narrower French alternative ('Ses droits et obligations de caractère civil') in establishing the scope of application of this Article.

Lord Wade's Bill has now, wisely, limited the parts of the European Convention to be incorporated to those which include the *operative* provisions of the Convention. Otherwise, at least technically, we should have had the rather remarkable position that the European Commission of Human Rights, as a body established as part of the framework of United Kingdom Law by Act of Parliament, would be amenable to the supervisory jurisdiction of the High Court in the exercise of its functions.

Even within the limited scope of Articles 1 to 18 and 60 of, and the first Protocol to, the Convention, a whole host of problems arises. For instance, Article 16 provides that nothing in certain other Articles of the Convention 'shall be regarded as preventing the High Contracting Parties from imposing restrictions on the political activity of aliens'. The state may act through any of its emanations and at many levels. Is it unreasonable to ask that an incorporating statute should indicate in what manner provisions limiting the political activities of aliens might be enacted without contravention of Article 16?

Many questions of interpretation would fall to be decided by a court, at considerable expense to some unfortunate litigant, but which could equally be determined one way or another in advance by Act of Parliament. It seems not to be unreasonable that some of these basic questions of interpretation should indeed be answered. For instance, is an application to commit to prison for contempt of court a criminal charge for the purposes of Article 6? The answer ought in my view to be yes, but the Phillimore Committee[4], although agreeing with the desirability of applying the standards of Article 6 as a test for the law of contempt, were unable to say authoritatively that Article 6 did apply to contempt of court.

Some of the answers to such questions may already have been given by the European Court of Human Rights, and it is important to decide what status the decisions of the latter should have in the courts of the United Kingdom. In my view, this existing case law should be accorded at least high persuasive authority. Since we are bound in international law by the relevant decisions of the Court of Human Rights, a strong case can be made for saying that our own courts should be bound by the Bill of Rights to follow these decisions in interpreting the Convention.

These points serve as a background for a more important point. Even an unentrenched Bill of Rights, if it is not totally anodyne, is likely to declare the existence of rights some of which existing legislation infringes. Whether for instance the Incitement to Disaffection Act 1934, or section 2 of the Official Secrets Act 1911, was incompatible with a Bill of Rights could only be finally determined by a court. Until that happened, the law would be in an undesirable state of uncertainty – undesirable especially in a field where the undecided question was whether particular conduct constituted an offence.

This may simply be regarded as one of those drawbacks of having a Bill of Rights that is part of the currency of arguments as to whether the idea is, on balance, desirable. But are there ways in which the uncertainty could be reduced? It would be possible to establish some official body – perhaps the Law Commissions would be suitable – to scrutinize the areas of the existing statute book most likely to give rise to questions, and to recommend amendments to legislation which could fall foul of a Bill of Rights, before the Bill was brought into effect. But apart from the massive nature of the task suggested, there are a number of possible drawbacks to this kind of approach. It is only in the forensic process that the issues on which a decision whether a particular right is infringed by legislation will become clear. There would also be a psychologically tempting argument, in subsequent cases, that existing legislation which had received a clean bill of health from this form of scrutiny must be taken as at least presumptively compatible with the Bill of Rights.

If the courts are to be given the task of declaring parts of statutes to be invalid, or of contorting their meaning in order to protect Parliament from the accident of infringing international obligations incorporated in the Bill of Rights, the least that Parliament can do is to make an effort to avoid creating legislation on which judges will have to perform this invidious surgery. This could be achieved by a form of pre-legislation scrutiny, within either Government Departments or Parliament, and perhaps a certificate from an appropriate body accompanying each Bill before it was allowed to proceed beyond a particular stage in the legislative process, to the effect that it appeared not to contravene the Bill of Rights.

Whether there should also be some mechanism for reference of more dubious legislative proposals to a judicial body for a determination of their compatibility with the Bill of Rights before enactment is a difficult question. Some such process was incorporated in the Scottish Devolution legislation, but it raises a considerable number of difficulties, not the least of which is that the decision would fall to be taken in the abstract. The same would be true of applications by individuals to the court for declarations of the invalidity of particular pieces of legislation. Recently, the House of Lords has indicated its dislike of applications by individuals for declarations that particular proposed forms of conduct do not constitute a criminal offence. Nevertheless, the most suitable way of airing an issue such as whether a newly-enacted criminal offence exists or not – putting graphically what this kind of judicial review involves – may be to apply for a declaration that the statutory provision creating the offence is not valid because it is neither expressed to take effect notwithstanding the Bill of Rights, nor incapable of being interpreted as compatible with it. Whatever the disadvantages of such an action, it has advantages for the individual whose freedom is infringed by the legislation over the alternative of taking the chance of being prosecuted and subjected to the risk of criminal penalties for conduct the legality of which is in dispute.

This leads me to one of the essential points about incorporation which has been neglected in much of the debate that has taken place. At the moment the protection of human rights is much more likely to be curtailed in practice for most individuals by inadequacies of the legal process than by substantive legislative intrusions on individual rights. Article 13 of the Convention recognises this by including the right to an 'effective remedy' among the rights guaranteed. The enactment of restraints on careless legislative intrusion on substantive rights ought in my view to be taken as an occasion for a general review of our procedures for securing redress for aggrieved individuals. The subject is a very large one, and to some extent independent of a Bill of Rights. But the fiction that judges merely declare what the law is, though wearing very thin, governs court procedures to a degree that could hardly be maintained were the judges openly required to decide what it should be – whether a particular restriction on freedom of speech was 'necessary in a democratic society', for instance. As the social consequences of decisions become unavoidably part of a judge's responsibilities, so the judge must be informed – not necessarily only by the parties – of what those consequences may be. Greater legal recognition of rights which do not have an obvious cash value puts a further strain on the rather limited concept of remedies under which we now operate: what remedies, for instance, should be available to a person prosecuted for an offence the existence of which violates rights guaranteed by the Convention?

We tend to think of remedies as being against the state or public authorities only, but private organisations and individuals may violate human rights, and remedies for such violations are just as important – intrusions by private security agents on rights of privacy are a clear example of a weakness in the present law. It is a point of controversy whether incorporation of the Convention would entitle individuals to make claims against other individuals; I suggest it would be desirable that there should be such a right, and the incorporating Act should – for the avoidance of doubt – say so specifically. Further, remedies by themselves are of little value unless people know of them and are able to pursue them. Enforcement agencies – with an important educative role – have been set up to complement individual rights to redress in most of our recent anti-discrimination legislation. Should this also be done for a Bill of Rights?

A final consideration is whether the very different and specialised questions likely to arise in the application and interpretation of a Bill of Rights justify the setting up of a special court to deal throughout the United Kingdom with such points as arise. (Until Scottish criminal appeals are allowed to be taken to the House of Lords we do not in the full sense have a United Kingdom Supreme Court.) Membership of a Constitutional Court would be but one of the difficult questions to be answered if the main question was answered in the affirmative

Dicey, with whose views I rarely agree, was right in one respect – in his argument that mere declarations of right are of much less value to the citizen than practical remedies. Traditionally, English Law has concerned itself with remedies rather than rights, but the remedies are too inaccessible, too expensive and sometimes not sufficiently flexible to meet modern needs. One of the most valuable functions of discussing a Bill of Rights is to highlight the opportunities that it throws open for a review of some of the weaknesses of legal procedure in fields outside the grounds of conventional litigation between private parties. The effective protection of human rights demands more than just a tablet of stone; steps need to be hewn out of the rock to the pinnacle on which the tablet is to be placed.

Part II

IRELAND, THE UNITED KINGDOM AND EMERGENCY CONDITIONS

In the first chapter Senator Mary Robinson offers an overview of the protection of rights in the Republic of Ireland. Her account of the adaptability of a system based on the common law to the introduction of a written Constitution is illuminating indicating the increasing creativity of judges in Ireland under the power of judicial review. Those who regard a written Constitution, or a written Bill of Rights, as anomalous to common law in England and Wales, for example, should gain insight from the Republic's history. Senator Robinson also outlines the emergency powers introduced and invoked over the decades – powers which in the international media often attract little attention as compared with the equivalents in Northern Ireland. The interplay between the written Constitution, entrenched rights and an emergency is described.

In Northern Ireland 'the troubles' have constituted a profound attack on the rule of law and its maintenance of freedom, order and control in society. The different views as to how the rights might best be protected in emergency conditions are discussed in the second chapter. Should there be a Charter of Rights for Northern Ireland? Or should any required reforms be for the United Kingdom as a whole? Should the administration of emergency powers be accountable only to Parliament or should there be a judicial review? The arguments in this chapter express unanimity on the need for law reform and unanimity that citizens in Northern Ireland need protection from the outrages of violence. There are differing views, however, as to what real lessons are to be learned from Northern Ireland and how the balance between order and liberty is to be maintained.

THE PROTECTION OF HUMAN RIGHTS IN THE REPUBLIC OF IRELAND

Senator Mary Robinson

The protection of human rights under the Irish Constitution of 1937 provides a fascinating subject in its own right. A major recent study[1] has revealed the extraordinary creativity of the Irish High Court and Supreme Court over the years, and the role which judges can play in ensuring the law reflects the needs and aspirations of citizens in a modern state. But rather than offer an essay on comparative law, my intention is to evaluate progress and performance in safeguarding human rights in that part of Ireland governed by a written Constitution. I shall focus on 'problem areas' including emergency legislation and the protection of minority rights.

The experience of a written Constitution

The Republic of Ireland provides an interesting model of a common law country adapting to a written Constitution. The Irish Free State inherited from Britain the fine tradition of the common law, and the basic organisation of the courts and the legal profession. But the Free State Constitution enacted in 1922 contained the elements of different constitutional developments. The very existence of a written Constitution, with guaranteed individual rights and a power of judicial review, meant that Dicey's views on the sovereignty of Parliament and the rule of law, had little relevance for the judges who now had to interpret this written Constitution and exercise the power of judicial review. However, the conditioning effect of a common law training and tradition left its mark. The transition by Irish judges to a recognition of the potential of a written Constitution for the protection of human rights was slow and even suspicious. Professor Kelly summed it up as follows:

> This function of reviewing legislation was one entirely new to the Irish judges of 1922 – the only judicial function even remotely similar had been the testing of administrative

measures for *vires* – and was one for which by their traditions and experience they were not very well conditioned. In the years 1922–1937 judicial interpretation of the Constitution played a very small part in the life of the State; and this is especially true of the fundamental rights provisions. The judges seem to have felt, for instance, that if freedom of speech existed, it was not primarily because the Constitution guaranteed it, but because – as in Britain – the ordinary law did not care what one said, provided that one's words were not an infraction of the ordinary law, e.g. by being seditious, blasphemous, slanderous or obscene, or by being a contravention of the Official Secrets Acts.[2]

By the time the present Constitution of Ireland was adopted in 1937, the Irish judiciary had become familiar with the function of judicial review and the interpretation of the articles in the Constitution guaranteeing fundamental rights. (The particular articles which detail such rights are Articles 40-44 covering personal rights, the family, education, rights of ownership, religious rights.) The Constitution (in Articles 46 and 47) provides for amendments to its provisions by the passage of a Bill and a referendum in which a majority of the people must approve the change. It also *expressly provides* for judicial review. The Oireachtas comprises the two Houses of the National Parliament – the Dail and the Seanad – and the President. Article 15 states the Oireachtas 'shall not enact any law which is in any respect repugnant to the Constitution' and further states any law which is enacted which is repugnant to the Constitution 'shall, but to the extent only of such repugnancy, be invalid'.

Article 34 confines the power to question the validity of a law under the provisions of the Constitution to the High Court and Supreme Court. Therefore, if an issue of validity of a law is raised in a lower court, that court may not deal with it; the matter must be brought before the High Court by way of declaratory action or in certain circumstances by an application for an Order of Certiorari. Apart from this power of judicial review, it is worth noting that the Supreme Court has a unique jurisdiction under Article 26 to pronounce on the compatibility with the Constitution of a Bill referred to it by the President before he signs it into law. If the Supreme Court decides that it is not compatible with the

Constitution then the President may not sign it.[3] This provision for reference of Bills to the Supreme Court does not apply to money Bills or Bills to amend the Constitution or urgent Bills where the time for consideration by the Seanad has been abridged.

It is understandable that judges trained in a common law tradition but faced with written guarantees of basic rights, and having the express power of judicial review, would turn away from the motherland of the common law and look elsewhere for inspiration in developing Irish constitutional law and theory. The Supreme Court of the United States is not the only external source from which Irish judges have borrowed, but it is certainly the most influential. The extent of the borrowing is illustrated by statistics relating to the reported Judgements of the Irish High Court and Supreme Court since 1937. These reveal that of a total of 139 reported cases on interpretation of the Constitution there were references to Supreme Court Judgments in 41, or almost one third. Indeed, this tendency to cite American authorities has become more marked in recent years, and has opened up a rich vein of judicial experience for Irish lawyers and judges interpreting the 1937 Constitution.

Was it any wonder, then, that a member of the Irish Supreme Court in a case in 1964 rejected the submission by Counsel for the Attorney-General that an English precedent be followed by remarking:

> The jurisdiction formerly enjoyed by the House of Lords in Ireland is but part of the much wider jurisdiction which has been conferred upon this court by the Constitution. I reject the submission that because upon the foundation of the State our courts took over an English legal system and the common law that the courts must be deemed to have adopted and should now adopt an approach to constitutional questions conditioned by English judicial methods and English legal training which despite their undoubted excellence were not fashioned for interpreting written constitutions or reviewing the constitutionality of legislation. In this State one would have expected that if the approach of any Court of final appeal of another State was to have been held up as an example for this Court to follow it would more appropriately have been the Supreme Court of

the United States rather than the House of Lords.[4]

It is generally agreed that the constitutional jurisprudence of the Irish courts since 1937 can be divided into two distinct phases –the first extends from 1938 to the mid-sixties, and the second from the mid-sixties to date. At first, the courts continued the cautious approach adopted under the Free State Constitution, but later there was an exciting period of judicial creativity under Chief Justice O'Dalaigh. The broader approach to interpretation of the Constitution subsists to the present day.

R. F. V. Heuston[5] discerns two distinct techniques of interpretation of the 1937 Constitution, a literal one according to which 'the Constitution must be interpreted from within its own four corners' and 'a very broad approach' which permits reference to the Preamble to the Constitution, to Article 45 concerning the directive principles of social policy which are intended for the general guidance of the Oireachtas, to the very nature of the Irish State, and even to the values expressed by the present Chief Justice O'Higgins in 1976:

> concepts of prudence, justice and charity which may gradually change or develop as society changes and develops, and which fall to be interpreted from time to time in accordance with prevailing ideas.[6]

In exercising their power of judicial review the Courts adopt a different approach to legislation which existed prior to the 1937 Constitution (which may or may not have been carried forward by the provisions of Article 50 of the 1937 Constitution) and post-1937 legislation which carries a presumption of constitutionality so that the Supreme Court has ruled that where two or more constructions of a statute are reasonably open, one being constitutional and the others not, the court will presume that the Oireachtas intended only the constitutional construction and uphold that construction. It is only when there is no construction reasonably open which is not repugnant to the Constitution that the provision should be held to be repugnant.[7]

One of the most interesting developments in recent years has been the identification of unspecified personal rights which the court is prepared to protect. Article 40.3.1 states:

The State guarantees in its laws to respect, and, as far as

practicable, by its laws to defend and vindicate the personal rights of the citizen.

The breakthrough came in 1963 in *Ryan v. A.-G.*[8] when a housewife objected to the fluoridation of the public water system contending that the relevant provisions of the Health (Fluoridation of Water Supplies) Act 1960 violated her constitutional rights. Mr Justice Kenny declared in the High Court that the Constitution required the protection not only of the rights *expressly* set out, but also other additional personal rights which would follow 'from the Christian and democratic nature of the State'. The Ryan case identified the right to bodily integrity, and since then there have been a number of unspecified rights which have either been upheld in constitutional actions or referred to by judges as coming within the personal rights under Article 40.3.1. The list includes: the right to dispose of and withdraw one's labour and the right not to belong to a trade union; the right to earn one's livelihood without discrimination; the right to work; the right to litigate claims; the right to prepare for and follow a chosen career; the right to be assisted by the State if one's health is in jeopardy; the right to marry; the right to free movement within the State; the right to marital privacy; the right to life, including the right of the foetus not to be aborted.

Apart from identifying such unspecified personal rights the courts have not hesitated to strike down legislation or to nullify procedures which infringed the constitutional rights of citizens. Some of these decisions will be referred to later, in the context of the protection of minority rights, but others include: declaring unconstitutional the system of voting at general elections, because it did not satisfy the constitutional standard of secrecy of the ballot; declaring unconstitutional the system for empanelling jurors under the Juries Act 1927, because it was discriminatory both on the basis of sex and by requiring a property qualification; declaring illegal the manner of dismissal of the Chief Commissioner of police because it contravened natural and constitutional justice; declaring unconstitutional a provision of the income tax code providing for the aggregation of the earned incomes of married couples for tax purposes, because it failed to protect marriage as required by Article 41. Professor Heuston remarks:

Very few doubts have been expressed, judicially or otherwise, on the point whether the Supreme Court may not have assumed too wide a jurisdiction. It is surprising to find so little political enmity towards the court on the part of members of the Oireachtas or administrators, because many of the court's decisions, e.g., that relating to the secret ballot, have been exceedingly inconvenient from an administrative point of view.[9]

A more trenchant viewpoint was expressed recently by another academic lawyer:

Constitutional review has been growing over the past fifteen years, to the accompaniment of an uncritical acclaim which may have been inspired by the mistaken notion that all movement is progress. It is high time that a more discerning interest is taken in the courts' activities. Otherwise, we may find that they have strayed even further beyond 'lawyers law' and taken to themselves more of the political decision-making power which is best exercised by the elected politicians.[10]

The erosion of written guarantees through emergency legislation and powers

Given the wide scope of emergency legislation in the Republic of Ireland, and the significant volume of such legislation since 1937, it is striking – not to say alarming – that there has been little research or monitoring of this legislation or its administration. There is little evidence of the 'constant vigilance' said to be one of the hallmarks of a democracy. The lack of parliamentary control and accountability in this area, reveals a political failure which has persisted over the years and indicates a weakness in the framework for the protection of human rights which has, as its basis, the written Constitution of 1937.

Although, as noted, the Constitution contains elaborate provisions in Articles 40 to 44 guaranteeing the protection of human rights, this does not prevent the enactment of far-reaching emergency legislation and substantial curtailment of judicial review. This is because Article 28.3.3 provides that:

Nothing in this Constitution shall be invoked to invalidate any law enacted by the Oireachtas which is expressed to be for the purpose of securing the public safety and the preservation of the State in time of war or armed rebellion, or to nullify any act done or purporting to be done in time of war or armed rebellion in pursuance of any such war.

Two amendments to this sub-section extended the expression 'time of war' to include an armed conflict in which the State was not a participant if the Houses of the Oireachtas resolved that it gave rise to a national emergency, and the duration of such emergency would include

such time after the termination of any war, or of any such armed conflict as aforesaid, or of an armed rebellion, as may elapse until each of the Houses of the Oireachtas shall have resolved the national emergency occasioned by such war, armed conflict, or armed rebellion has ceased to exist.

In effect, this sub-section excludes judicial review of emergency legislation enacted while there is a resolution of the Oireachtas declaring a state of national emergency. The problem is that a State of Emergency has existed for practically the entire period of the 1937 Constitution! The Oireachtas passed a resolution under Article 28.3.3 on 2 September 1939 and this resolution was not repealed until 1 September 1976, when it was replaced by a new resolution as follows:

Dial Eireann hereby resolves, pursuant to sub-section 3 of section 3 of Article 28 of the Constitution that, arising out of the armed conflict now taking place in Northern Ireland, a National Emergency exists affecting the vital interests of the State.

On the basis of this resolution, the Emergency Powers Bill 1976 was passed enabling persons to be held in custody without charge for a maximum period of seven days. This Bill was referred by the President to the Supreme Court under Article 26 of the Constitution, and whilst upholding the constitutionality of the Bill (which subsequently became law) the Supreme Court laid down some important qualifications on the scope of the resolution.

. . . when a law is saved from invalidity by Article 28, Section 3, sub-section (3), the prohibition against invoking the Constitution in reference to it is only if the invocation is for the purpose of invalidating it. For every other purpose the

Constitution may be invoked. Thus, a person detained under section 2 of the Bill may not only question the legality of his detention if there has been non-compliance with the express requirements of section 2, but may also rely on provisions of the Constitution for the purpose of construing that section and of testing the legality of what has been done in purported operation of it. A statutory provision of this nature which makes such inroads upon the liberty of the person must be strictly construed . . . the section is not to be read as an abnegation of the arrested person's rights, constitutional or otherwise, in respect of matters such as the right of com-munication, the right to have legal and medical assistance, and the right of access to the Courts. If the section were used in breach of such rights the High Court might grant an order for release under the provisions for *habeas corpus* contained in the Constitution.[11]

Declarations of Emergency and of need for Special Powers

The mechanisms for declaring a state of emergency, or for invoking full powers under emergency legislation are complex and sophisticated. As mentioned, there is the power under Article 28.3.3 of the Constitution for both Houses of the Oireachtas to resolve that an emergency exists. However, the Emergency Powers Act 1976 provided a trigger mechanism of its own: that the powers in that Act, including the power to detain without charge for up to seven days, would only continue in force for a year unless renewed by Government Order. In October 1977 the Government announced that it did not then propose to make a further Order, so the powers under the Act lapsed. However, the Act provides that the powers may be re-invoked at any time by order of the Government; any such Order must be laid before the Oireachtas and may be annulled by motion passed to that effect within twenty-one sitting days. The reality of course is that the Government of the day has a majority in both Houses, so it is not politically realistic to envisage a motion annulling a Government Order. Consequently, and Government may, by Order, re-invoke the full powers conferred under the Emergency Powers Act 1976. By not repealing the Act, or declaring that the State of Emergency was at an end (in which case the Act itself would have lapsed), the Government have continued discretion

to re-introduce emergency powers whenever the Executive
deems it necessary.

A similar mechanism is contained in the Offences Against the
State Act 1939 with regard to the establishment of special courts
to try serious criminal offences without a jury, and also under the
Offences Against the State (Amendment) Act 1940 for the
introduction of internment. In both cases all that is required is a
Government declaration, and no direct involvement by the
Oireachtas. Section 35(1) of the 1939 Act reproduces the
provision of Article 38.3.1 of the Constitution which provides
that:

> If and whenever and so often as the Government is satisfied
> that the ordinary courts are inadequate to secure the effective
> administration of justice and the preservation of public peace
> and order and that it is therefore necessary that this part of this
> Act should come into force, the Government may make and
> publish a proclamation declaring that the Government is
> satisfied as aforesaid and ordering that this part of this Act
> shall come into force.

Section 35(5) of the 1939 Act provides that the Dail may by
resolution annul such a proclamation – alternatively the
Government may by further order declare that the ordinary
courts are no longer inadequate.

A similar mechanism existed in Part VI of the 1939 Act for
introducing internment, but following a successful *habeas corpus*
case on the power given to a Minister under section 55 of that
Act, the Offences Against the State (Amendment) Bill 1940 was
introduced, referred to the Supreme Court under Article 26 and
upheld by the Supreme Court. This provides that once the
Government has declared the provisions of the Bill are necessary
'to secure the preservation of public peace and order', a person
can be interned

> whenever a Minister of State is of the opinion that any
> particular person is engaged in activities calculated to prejudice
> the preservation of the peace, order, or security of the State,
> such Minister may by warrant under his hand order the arrest
> and detention of such person under this section . . .

It was this provision which was challenged before the European

Court of Human Rights which concluded that

> In conclusion, the Irish Government were justified in declaring that there was a public emergency in the Republic of Ireland threatening the life of the nation and were hence entitled, applying the provisions of Article 15(1) of the Convention for the purposes for which those provisions were made, to take measures derogating from their obligations under the Convention.[12]

Emergency legislation can therefore be construed narrowly as the legislation which comes precisely within the provisions of Article 28.3.3 which allows a derogation from the protection afforded by the 1937 Constitution, and such legislation has to be expressed to be 'for the purpose of securing the public safety and the preservation of the State in time of war or armed rebellion'; or the term may be read in a less technical sense to include legislation giving extensive powers of law enforcement and establishing special courts under Article 38.3 of the 1937 Constitution. It is in this broader sense that I classify measures as being 'emergency legislation', because in intent and purpose and in granting wide powers to law enforcement agencies, the scope of personal liberty and the protection of human rights is limited.

The main statutes in force which can thus be classed as emergency legislation are the Offences Against the State Act 1939, the Offences Against the State (Amendment) Act 1940, the Offences Against the State (Amendment) Act 1972, the Criminal Law Act 1976, the Emergency powers Act 1976, and the Criminal Law (Jurisdiction) Act 1976. Rather than examining the Acts (as amended) one by one let me draw attention to the more important areas and indicate the legal position – this may help us to assess realistically the impact on individual human rights.

Membership of an unlawful organisation

Section 21 of the Offences Against the State Act 1939 created the offence of membership of an unlawful organisation and provided a maximum penalty of two years imprisonment. This has been increased by the Criminal Law Act 1976 to a maximum penalty of seven years; and the 1976 Act created a new offence – carrying a maximum penalty of ten years – of recruitment etc. for an unlawful organisation. Section 3 of the Offences Against the State (Amendment) Act 1972 made a significant change in the nature of the evidence which could be produced in court to establish membership of an unlawful organisation. Sub-section (1) provided that:

> Any statement made orally, in writing or otherwise, or any conduct, by an accused person implying or leading to a reasonable inference that he was at a material time a member of an unlawful organisation shall, in proceedings under section 21 of the Act of 1939, be evidence that he was then such a member.

It also provides that the word 'conduct' includes omission by the accused person to deny published reports that he was a member of an unlawful organisation, although the fact of such denial shall not by itself be conclusive. Concern was expressed by the press about the dangers inherent in such extension of the normal meaning of the word 'conduct', and the effect it might have on the freedom of the press.

Section 3(2) of the 1972 Act made a conviction possible on the sole evidence of a Garda Superintendent if he 'states that he believes that the accused was at a material time a member of an unlawful organisation (then) the statement shall be evidence that he was . . . such a member.'[13]

This section was strongly criticised in the debates in both the Dail and Senate, and by outside commentators. Various dangers were pointed out. The way in which information is gathered by intelligence services in any country is open to error; to allow such information to have the status of 'evidence', and then protect the witness from cross examination (by allowing the Superintendent to plead privilege) creates an extremely dangerous precedent. In effect, this would not even be a case of one man's word against another, but a case of a *belief* based on undivulged material derived from undivulged sources – which could be at second or third hand – being set against another man's assertions. In practice, if an accused either states on oath or even makes an unsworn statement that he is not, or was not at the material time, a member of the IRA then this raises a doubt in the minds of the judges of the court, and the accused is given the benefit of that doubt.

Powers of arrest and detention

Section 30 of the Offences Against the State Act 1939 deals with powers of arrest and detention without warrant of anyone suspected of an offence under that Act or a scheduled offence, or anyone suspected of being in possession of information relating to such offences. Section 30 (3) allows a person to be held in custody for twenty-four hours – and for a further period of twenty-four hours if a Garda officer not below the rank of Chief Superintendent so directs. If not charged before the District Court or Special Criminal Court, the accused must be released after the forty-eight-hour period. The Emergency Powers Act 1976 (referred by President O'Dalaigh to the Supreme Court as a Bill under Article 26 of the Constitution) provided for the detention of a person for a further five days following the period of forty-eight hours – a total of seven days detention. As mentioned, the 1976 Act has not been repealed, but the Government in 1977 did not renew the Order which permits the holding of suspects for up to seven days without charge. However the power to reintroduce the provisions by Government Order is still on the stocks, and the declaration of emergency which entitled the Government in 1976 to introduce the Emergency Powers Bill remains in effect.

The summer of 1976 offers an interesting case study of a Government under stress. There is no doubt the threat posed by the use of violence and terrorism by unlawful organisations is difficult to combat in a democratic society. Yet in August 1976 it appeared, when the Houses of the Oireachtas were specially reconvened, that the Coalition Government was in danger of losing its nerve and judgment. In the debate about a new declaration of emergency and the Emergency Powers Act 1976, the statement by the Minister for Justice is revealing:

> In the Government's view, the situation requires that the Government should be able to take emergency powers to whatever extent may be necessary to crush the armed conspiracy against lives and democratic government which faces the nation . . . It is our wish and our intention to proceed at all times in accordance with the rule of law. But the very existence in the Constitution of the Article under which this resolution is moved is evidence that there are circumstances in

which a democratic government may be compelled to limit the exercise of individual rights in the interest of protecting from attack the ordered community of the State, without which anarchy and armed repression would reign supreme and the exercise of individual rights and fundamental freedoms be utterly abolished.[14]

It is worth noting the powers of the Garda Siochana in relation to persons arrested under section 30 of the 1939 Act (and section 2 of the 1976 Act while in force). Under section 7 of the Criminal Law Act 1976 a member of the Garda may demand the name and address of the person, take his fingerprints and palm prints; he may also make any test designed to ascertain whether there has been contact with any firearm or explosive substance; and he may seize and retain for testing anything that the person has in his possession.

Impact of emergency legislation

The Republic of Ireland has suffered much less severe strain and direct attack from the activities of members of unlawful groups prepared to use violence to achieve their political aims than has Northern Ireland. However, the approach of successive governments has been to ensure the maximum power to cope with any emergency situation is held in reserve – and can be brought into full effect by *executive* action. Surprisingly, there has been relatively little criticism of this *de facto* increase in executive power, and almost no research into its broader implications. The danger of such bland acceptance of a state of emergency has been summed up by O'Boyle writing in the context of Northern Ireland.

> Perhaps the most dangerous risk of all concerns the impact of emergency legislation on the nature of government and the political morality of society. The frequent use of emergency powers to cope with crises, coupled with the success of these powers, acclimatises administrators to their use, and makes recourse to them in the future, all the easier. The danger is, that succeeding generations of administrators inherit these powers as being efficient and unobjectionable, and in a particular emergency, do not give proper consideration to the possibility of less drastic measures being used. In addition,

social attitudes develop so as to accept recourse to emergency measures as the norm and over time there grows an insensitivity to the human rights problems that are inevitably associated with public emergencies . . . there exists the danger that an over zealous use of emergency powers can promote a lack of confidence in the security forces and a counter-productive alienation of a wide section of society. If this occurs, then the use of emergency powers exacerbates the problem they were designed to cure.[15]

The Special Criminal Court[16]

In 1974, I conducted a limited examination of the Special Criminal Court.[17] This included analysis of the constitutional and legal authority for the Special Criminal Courts, a description of the earlier Special Criminal Court set up in August 1939, and an assessment of the workload of the present Court. I made five specific recommendations:

1 The sections of the Offences Against the State Act 1939 which appear open to constitutional attack should be repealed;
2 Amending legislation should be introduced to give the Oireachtas control over the establishment and functioning of the Special Criminal Court. The Government should not be able to act by proclamation without reference to the Oireachtas. Ministerial Orders scheduling offences for the purposes of Part 5 of the Act should be laid before the Oireachtas subject to annulment. A time limit should be placed on the functioning of a particular special criminal court when established;
3 In view of the dual function of the Special Criminal Court, and the need for high judicial standards, the membership of any such Special Criminal Court should be confined to members of the judiciary;
4 Sittings of the Special Criminal Court should be presided over in so far as possible by a High Court Judge;
5 Since the Special Criminal Court is a truly indigenous development, and does not derive from the common law, it must be scrutinised with care to ensure that it does not make any unjustifiable inroads on the right to trial by jury. An independent enquiry should establish whether, as alleged, persons have been tried before the present Special Criminal

Court who had no connection with any unlawful organisation or subversive group.

Sadly, these major criticisms still appear to be valid, and, six years later, there has not been any substantial enquiry (either Governmental or independent) into the operation of the Special Criminal Court. (The DPP now exercises the functions of the Attorney General, under the Prosecution of Offences Act 1974, and in practice the Court has been presided over by a High Court Judge and its membership is confined to members of the judiciary.) The statistics indicate that from June 1972 to the end of 1979, there were 1,044 persons convicted and 386 acquitted and the sentences meted out to those convicted make a convincing case that further study and analysis is required.[18]

Lack of Parliamentary control

It is a precondition to the lawful establishment of Special Courts that the ordinary courts are found to be inadequate, and a condition of their validity that this inadequacy continues throughout their duration. This ought to place a burden of responsibility on the Oireachtas to monitor the situation closely, and to determine whether in fact the ordinary courts *remain* inadequate for the administration of justice in certain circumstances. At the moment the Oireachtas shirks this responsibility, and the Government is under no statutory obligation to account for the continuance in force of the declaration under Part 5 of the 1939 Act authorising the establishment of the Court. The absence of monitoring by the Oireachtas and accountability by the Government has resulted in a serious implication which is certainly not in the spirit of Article 38 of the Constitution. It creates the impression – never intended by the Constitution – that the Special Criminal Court is part of the ordinary administration of justice and has become a permanent fixture in the judicial structure.

Moreover, there is a specific constitutional duty arising from the words of Article 40.3.1 to the effect that 'The State guarantees in its laws to respect, and, as far as possible, by its laws to defend and vindicate the personal rights of the citizen.' How has this duty been discharged over the past 7½ years in so far as it requires the State to defend and vindicate the personal right to trial by jury? Can the State be satisfied that not one of the 1,500 or so persons tried by that Court was deprived of the personal right to trial by jury in circumstances where the ordinary courts would have been perfectly adequate? Does the machinery under Part 5 of the Offences Against the State Act 1939 satisfy the basic standard of vigilance for the personal rights of citizens required by the Constitution?

At the very least, there should be an annual report laid by the Minister for Justice before the Oireachtas which would contain a statistical profile of the case-load of the Court, and a statement by the Government of the grounds on which it was considered necessary to continue the Special Criminal Court in existence for a further year. Deputies should not have to rely on individual Parliamentary Questions, or on the debate on the Estimates of the Department of Justice, as the sole means of eliciting unrelated items of information about the operation of this exceptional court.

Isolation of Special Criminal Court

Although the Special Criminal Court now tends to be regarded as a permanent fixture in the administration of justice, it is not fully integrated into the legal system and does not benefit from the safeguards and standards which might result if it were. There are several reasons for this. The first stems from the physical location of the Court. The Special Criminal Court is located far enough away from the Four Courts to deter casual attendance by barristers who are accustomed to sitting in on cases of interest in the High Court or Supreme Court.

Second, and more seriously, there is evidence that a very small number of barristers appear regularly before the Special Criminal Court. The number of Senior Counsel appearing for the prosecution is less than ten out of a potential pool of over fifty. On the defence side it would be less than five. The Bar Council has not troubled to attempt to ensure a representative panel of Senior Counsel is available and willing to take cases, for either prosecution or defence, before the Court. Meanwhile, the isolation becomes greater, increasing the concern that a barrister offered a brief to appear in that Court might decline because he lacked experience and regarded the Special Criminal Court as somehow 'different' or even 'alien'.

Third, the Special Criminal Court is left outside the regular system of law reporting under the auspices of the Incorporated Council of Law Reporting for Ireland. That body assigns barristers as reporters of cases in the High Court and Supreme Court. It is their reports which comprise the official Irish Reports. As there is no reporter assigned to the Special Criminal Court, no ruling of that Court in almost eight years has been reported in the Irish Reports. Also, since the judgments of the Special Criminal Court tend to be given orally, it can be difficult to obtain copies of the judgments either for the use of practitioners or for research. (A shorthand note is taken in every case, but a transcript is prepared only in the case of an appeal: in the absence of an appeal the notes are virtually inaccessible.) This is all the more regrettable given the very wide jurisdiction of the Special Criminal Court – not only is it a trial court for criminal cases, but it also has an important jurisdiction in bail applications and a jurisdiction equivalent to that of the District Court in preliminary examinations of indictable offences. How strange, then, that not a single ruling of the Court has found its way into the official reports of Irish cases!

Jurisprudence of the Special Criminal Court

In the absence of any reported cases, it is rather difficult to assess the developing jurisprudence of the Court. While there may be an appeal to the Court of Criminal Appeal, no appeal will be allowed from findings of fact. In so far as judgments of the Special Criminal Court are confined to findings of fact and do not elaborate on points of law, this can therefore effectively deprive an accused of a right of appeal. Without detailed research no firm conclusions can be reached on this point.

Some of the more important decisions of the Special Criminal Court are referred to in the O'Briain Report published in 1978. Reference is made to *The People v. Stenson* 1977 (unreported) in which the President of the High Court rejected the concept of detention by the Gardai short of actual arrest, the purpose of which was to enable the police to pursue enquiries to gather evidence. Another important decision clarifying the right of access to a solicitor was given by the same judge in *Harrington's Case* in 1976, but this time sitting as a judge of the High Court in a *habeas corpus* Application. However, given the volume of cases, and the wide jurisdiction of the Court, it is surprising not to have a richer storehouse of jurisprudence on which to draw.

Admissibility of statements

A continuing problem for the Special Criminal Court is the significant number of cases which depend for convictions on the admissibility of oral or written confessions by the accused. Allegations of intimidation or abuse of persons held in custody give rise to two kinds of concern: alarm at the possibility of such abuse, and worry that if allegations are unfounded but uninvestigated they may nonetheless prove damaging to the reputation of the Gardai.

Over the past eight years there have been periods when very serious allegations of abuse of persons held in custody were made, and a 'heavy gang' was identified as carrying the main responsibility. The first formal investigation came from an outside body, Amnesty International. In 1977 the Amnesty Report was made public by the Government, but with the significant omission of the section which made criticisms of the Special Criminal Court. However, this section was printed in full in *The Irish Times* on the same day, and contained the following passage:

> The Special Criminal Court has rarely dismissed a case on the grounds that the prosecution failed to establish beyond doubt that statements were voluntary but has thus far appeared consistently to accept police testimony as against that of the accused. From an examination of several cases appearing before the Special Criminal Court in the past it appears to Amnesty International that, despite the standards proclaimed by the former Minister for Justice, the onus of proof has in effect ben on the defence to establish beyond all reasonable doubt that maltreatment did occur, rather than on the prosecution to prove that it did not.[19]

Immediately afterwards the O'Briain Committee was established by the Government.

O'Briain Report and Recommendations

The terms of reference for the committee were two-fold:

To recommend with all convenient speed whether, and if so, what additional safeguards are necessary or desirable for the protection against ill-treatment of persons in Garda custody, having regard to allegations made in relation to persons held in such custody pursuant to section 30 of the Offences Against the State Act 1939, or section 2 of the Emergency Powers Act 1976, and for the protection of members of the Garda Siochana against unjustified allegations of such ill-treatment; and for that purpose to seek such information as would be likely to be of assistance to them in making a recommendation as aforesaid. The proceedings of the committee will be private and their report will be made to the Government.

The Report was presented to the Government in April 1978, and subsequently published. It contained a number of important recommendations for safeguards for persons held in custody, most notably the appointment in each case of a custodial guardian, but this and other important recommendations were rejected by the Government. However, there has been some improvement. A form has been introduced which the Gardai are required to complete in each case – accounting for the where-abouts of the accused, who interviewed him and for how long, what food he ate, what visitors he had, whether seen by solicitor, doctor, etc. Also there appears to have been a healthy shift of emphasis away from reliance solely on confessions to forensic evidence. The Department of Justice has been given greater facilities and staff, so that now it can produce highly sophisticated tests and evidence for use before the Court. It would be interesting to know whether or not this has affected the number of verbal confessions or written statements by persons held in custody. Alas, the research needed to draw such inferences is non-existent.

Conclusion

Six years ago the need for research was obvious. Now it is a matter of scandal, and an indictment of the academic law shools for failing to effect a thorough examination of the Special Criminal Court. Indeed, might there not be particular value in *comparative* research into the operation of that Court and the Diplock Courts in Northern Ireland? Such a study could even investigate whether the Diplock Courts, operating in a divided community, are under greater pressure to 'provide rationality' than the Special Criminal Court tucked away in the recesses of a more homogeneous and less questioning society.

The problem of updating a written Constitution

There are a number of advantages in having a written Constitution with an express power of judicial review by the courts. There is also the problem of amending that Constitution if it contains provisions which no longer reflect current social or political values, or which are seen as oppressive of minorities in the community. Article 46 of the 1937 Constitution deals with amendment, and requires that a Bill be introduced in the Dail and passed by both Houses, and then approved in a referendum by a simple majority of those voting. There have been seven Acts to amend the 1937 Constitution, and two Bills which sought to change the method of voting from proportional representation to direct voting which, although proposed by the Fianna Fail party when in government, failed to secure the necessary majority.

The Acts to amend the Constitution include the following: the removal of the reference to the special position of the Catholic Church in Article 41; the reduction of the voting age in parliamentary elections to 18; the insertion of a provision enabling Ireland to join the European Communities; and two Acts voted on by referendum in June 1979 on two separate issues – relating to the constitutionality of the Adoption Board's powers, and the method of representation of universities etc. in the Senate.

In 1967 an all-party committee reported on areas of the Constitution which might require amendment.[20] The report is interesting because some of its recommendations appear to go further than would now be possible on an all-party basis. For example, the committee was prepared to recommend an amendment of Article 3 of the Constitution which at present provides as follows:

Pending the re-integration of the national territory, and without prejudice to the right of the Parliament and Government established by this Constitution to exercise jurisdiction over the whole of that territory, the laws enacted by that Parliament shall have the like area and extent of application as the laws of Saorstat Eireann and the like extra-territorial effect.

The 1967 all-party committee recommended that a new provision be adopted to replace Article 3 as follows:

> 1 The Irish nation hereby proclaims its firm will that its territory be re-united in harmony and brotherly affection between all Irishmen.
> 2 The laws enacted by the Parliament established by this Constitution shall, until the achievement of the nation's unity shall otherwise require, have the like area and extent of application as the laws of the Parliament which existed prior to the adoption of this Constitution. Provision may be made by law to give extra-territorial effect to such laws.

The Committee did not explain why it made this recommendation, but the fact that an all-party committee could agree to any modification of Article 3 in 1967 is interesting in itself. It is to be doubted whether such a bipartisan approach could operate now, given the polarising effects of events in the past decade.

Divorce

Another sensitive issue, now under active discussion in the Republic, is the prohibition on any divorce law contained in Article 41.3 of the Constitution. The main problem is that any change requires a Bill to amend the Constitution, and the approval of that Bill by a majority of voters in a referendum. Recently a Divorce Action Group was formed to lobby for an amendment to the Constitution, and an updating of the marriage law in Ireland. This Group intends to form local groups, gather statistical information, and increase awareness of the problems, the oppression and misery caused by the present absolute prohibition. The Labour Party has accepted as party policy, the need to amend the Constitution to allow divorce law, and it is to be hoped that a Bill to that effect may be tabled by the Parliamentary Labour Party in the near future.

Abortion

There is increasing concern in the Republic of Ireland at the sharp rise in the numbers of women who travel to the United

Kingdom to obtain abortions, either on the National Health Service or in private clinics. Abortion is illegal in the Republic, and the criminal penalties have remained unchanged since the Offences Against the Person Act 1861. As yet the issue of abortion has not been raised directly before the Irish courts. However, there are some judicial dicta which appear to close the door to any approach to the issue similar to that adopted by the United States Supreme Court.

The first case was the *McGee Case* in 1974 in which the provision of a criminal Act in 1935 prohibiting the importation of contraceptives for private use, was declared unconstitutional. In that case the Supreme Court had cited with approval *Griswold v. Connecticut*, but Mr Justice Walsh seemed wary of the link between that case and the subsequent decision of *Roe v. Wade* in 1972 which recognised a right of personal privacy protected by the due process clause that included a qualified right of a woman to determine whether to bear a child or not. In his judgment he appeared eager to preclude any development from the principles in the *McGee Case* to a right to abortion under Irish law. In a key passage he stated as follows:

> . . . to limit family sizes by endangering or destroying human life must necessarily not only be an offence against the common good but also against the guaranteed personal rights of the human life in question.[21]

The Judge did not go on to define 'human life' in this context, but in a more recent case on adoption, *G. v. Adoption Board* in 1979, he cited the passage quoted and continued:

> The child's natural rights spring primarily from the natural right of every individual to life, to be reared and educated, to liberty, to work, to rest and recreation, to the practice of religion and to follow his or her conscience. The right to life necessarily implies the right to be born, the right to preserve and defend, and to have preserved and defended, that life, and the right to maintain that life at a proper human standard in matters of food, clothing and habitation. It lies not in the power of the parent who has the primary natural rights and duties in respect of the child to exercise them in such a way as intentionally or by neglect to endanger the health or life of the

child or to terminate its existence. The child's natural right to life and all that flows from that right are independent of any right of the parent as such.[22]

Right to use contraceptives

The role of the Irish courts in protecting individual rights is illustrated by the long drawn out struggle in the 1970s for legalisation of the sale and importation of contraceptives. Section 17 of the Criminal Law (Amendment) Act 1935 prohibited the sale, advertising or importation either for sale or private use of contraceptive devices. In 1971 a Private Member's Bill seeking to amend the section was refused a First Reading in the Senate. A second Private Member's Bill obtained a First Reading in 1973. Meanwhile, an action had been taken in the High Court by Mrs McGee, claiming a declaration that the provisions of section 17 contravened her constitutional rights, and in particular her right to marital privacy. The action failed in the High Court, but succeeded on appeal to the Supreme Court which handed down its decision in December 1973.[23] Because the 1935 Act pre-dated the Constitution, the effect of the Court's decision was to rule that the sub-section of section 17 of that Act which prohibited the importation of contraceptives for private use was not carried forward by Article 50 of the 1937 Constitution.[24]

Despite this breakthrough, the Private Member's Bill was defeated and a measure proposed by the Coalition Government (The Control of Importation, Sale and Manufacture of Contraceptives Bill 1974) was defeated in 1974 when the then Taoiseach and Minister for Education (and other Government deputies) crossed the floor to ensure its defeat. Two other Private Members' Bills were introduced, the Family Planning Bill in 1974 and the Family Planning Bill 1978[25], but it was not until 1979 that a Government Bill, the Health (Family Planning) Bill 1979, was passed. However, at the time of writing, this Act has still not been brought into effect, and its provisions remain suspended pending the enactment of regulations by the Minister for Health.

Meanwhile, the courts were involved in another action brought by the Irish Family Planning Association against the Irish Censorship Board, to challenge the ban on their explanatory booklets on family planning. This action succeeded in the High Court and was upheld by the Supreme Court in 1978.[26] Although the constitutionality of the powers of the Censorship Board had been challenged on the grounds that they failed to respect citizens' rights 'to express their convictions and opinions' and to 'impart information and ideas without interference by public authority subject to public order and morality', neither Court found it necessary to consider these issues; they held against the Board on the narrower grounds that it had contravened the principles of natural and constitutional justice.

Married taxation

In a recent decision the Supreme Court declared unconstitutional, as contravening the special protection of the family guaranteed under Article 41 of the Constitution, the aggregation of the earned incomes of married couples for tax purposes.[27] It had long been felt that the language of Article 41, which speaks of the fact that 'the State recognises that by her life within the home, woman gives to the State a support without which the common good cannot be achieved' would be a deterrent to the protection of the right of married women to seek employment. However, this view was rejected by the Supreme Court, which in effect decided that the State had to guard with special care the institution of marriage – this included ensuring that married couples suffered no financial disadvantages under the tax code.

Religious discrimination

Article 44 prohibits religious endowment or discrimination by the State. Article 44.2 provides:
   (ii) the State guarantees not to endow any religion
   (iii) the State shall not impose any disabilities or make any
        discrimination on the grounds of religious profession,
        belief or status.
These provisions have been considered in a number of important constitutional cases, including one where a priest claimed the rules for the payment of incremental salary to teachers were discriminatory, because the incremental credit for teaching in Third World countries applied only to recognised lay teachers. The priest succeeded in establishing that this amounted to a discrimination based on a difference in religious status which

was contrary to Article 44.[28]

In another case the provision of section 12 of the Adoption Act 1952 which prohibited adoption by parties to a 'mixed marriage' was challenged successfully in the High Court as being in contravention of Article 44.2.3.[29] The State did not appeal against this decision and shortly afterwards the Adoption Act 1974 was enacted providing for adoption by adoptive parents of different religions provided that this situation was known and consented to by the person placing the child for adoption.

A case which *failed* to establish discrimination on the ground of religious status, and in which the Supreme Court adopted the view that the prohibition of religious discrimination affects only the State, was an action brought by two members of staff against the Trustees of Maynooth College.[30] Both men were priests. One had become laicised and the other had indicated an intention to become laicised, when they were dismissed for alleged breaches of College Statutes. They argued that their dismissal resulted essentially from the steps taken to become laicised, and as such it represented a 'discrimination on the ground of religious status' contrary to Article 44.2.3. However, the Court rejected this submission, and confined the prohibition in Article 44 to the State and not to other persons or bodies even those in receipt of a subvention from the State as was Maynooth College. This appears to be the first case challenging discrimination by a non-State body and also involving the question whether a State-subvention to a religious seminary was unconstitutional. Similar issues are involved in a current debate on Deeds of Trust for Community Schools in the Republic, where the model Deed of Trust (accepted by the Minister and approved by a number of Vocational Education Committees) contains provisions for reserved places for members of religious orders both when the community school is established and for the future.

Family rights

One of the most worrying developments in the interpretation by the courts of the Constitution, is the confinement of family rights under Articles 41 and 42 to the family founded on the institution of marriage. The first case was *State (Nicolaou) v. Adoption Board*[31], an action brought by the natural father of a child who had been placed in adoption against his wishes. The Supreme

Court concluded that it was quite clear that the family referred to in Article 41 'is the family which is founded on the institution of marriage and, in the context of the Article, marriage means valid marriage under the law for the time being in force in the State . . .'

This case has been cited and approved in a number of cases concerning the rights, or rather lack of family rights, of natural parents. In the recent important case of *G v. Adoption Board*[32], the five judges of the Supreme Court divided three to two on the question as to whether an unmarried mother had a personal right under the Constitution to the custody and care of her child or only legislative rights under the Guardianship of Infants Act 1964. Three of the judges upheld her personal rights under Article 40, section 3, whereas the other two judges were of the opinion that an unmarried mother had no constitutional rights but only legislative rights in relation to her child.

It may be that the lack of constitutional rights, and the poor protection under legislation of a natural father could give rise to an application to the European Commission on Human Rights that the treatment of natural fathers under the Irish Constitution and law is in breach of the European Convention on Human Rights and Fundamental Freedoms. Certainly, the confinement of the identification of family rights under the Constitution to the family based on a valid marriage, raises complex issues in a State which prohibits in its Constitution the legal dissolution of a marriage.

Civil legal aid and advice

One important aspect of the protection of human rights is the guarantee of access to the courts and to justice. The absence of any state scheme of civil legal aid in the Republic undoubtedly deprived some citizens of this basic right, and led to a finding by the European Court of Human Rights in the *Airey Case* that Ireland was in breach of Articles 6 and 8 of the European Convention.[33] A system of criminal legal aid has been in operation since 1965, and in December 1979 the Government published details of a scheme for civil legal aid and advice which it proposed to implement during 1980.

Conclusion

The purpose of this paper has been to examine the implications

for a common law country of the enactment of a written
Constitution containing express power of judicial review.

It is clear that the power to derogate from the written
guarantees in the Irish Constitution of 1937 is very wide, and
that this power has been exercised in such a way as to create a
technical state of emergency which has lasted for over forty
years. Successive governments have been able to operate in this
way because of the absence of insistence upon strict scrutiny by
and accountability to the national parliament, and because of a
lack of effective monitoring and vigilance by academic lawyers
and concerned citizens. However, although the constitutional
guarantees have been weakened in practice, the Irish courts have
nevertheless exercised an important and continuing role in
identifying and protecting the rights of individuals.

Another characteristic of the Republic since the enactment of
the 1937 Constitution has been an absence of concern for
legislative reform, particularly in areas where the law encroaches
on the private morality of citizens. This may be explained to
some extent by the predominance of Roman Catholicism as the
religion of some 95% of the population, and the consequent
difficulty of asserting minority rights and the need to create a
basic framework appropriate to a pluralist society. In the
absence of legislative initiative, there has been a tendency for test
cases to be brought in the High Court seeking declarations either
that laws which pre-dated the Constitution were not carried
forward by Article 50 because they were repugnant to it, or that
laws enacted by the Oireachtas since 1937 contravened the basic
rights of citizens. Indeed, it might be said that there is a direct
relation between the creativity of the Irish judiciary in constitutional cases and the inactivity and neglect of the legislature
particularly in areas such as family law reform.

This raises broader political questions: whether such a relationship is a healthy one in a democratic society? Whether politicians
may in fact avoid facing up to their legislative responsibility if
they can rely on court cases to bring about certain changes?
Whether constitutional review is an appropriate instrument for
effecting social and economic change? Providing the answers
could well be the subject of an entirely different analysis!

VIOLENCE AND HUMAN RIGHTS IN NORTHERN IRELAND

The hostile environment: *Professor C. M. Campbell*

Discussions about human rights in Northern Ireland are fraught with difficulties. The controversy and the publicity about Northern Ireland – the violence, the politics and possible constitutional solutions – have militated against rational and calm discourse. In Britain, Western Europe and in North America even casual conversations about Northern Ireland quickly reveal deep-rooted prejudices and antagonisms, and often provoke emotional reactions. Even in Northern Ireland itself, and in the Republic of Ireland, talking about 'the troubles' can seem tendentious. The historical developments which led to partition and the different versions of the rights and wrongs of earlier centuries, bear down on almost all people in a stifling fashion. Sometimes it is demanded that any statement about current issues must be presaged by an account of developments from the sixteenth century onwards.

Yet even if historical analyses and proposals for constitutional settlements were within my competence – which they are not – I would suggest they can be set to one side, in some ways at least, in examining the protection of human rights by law in Northern Ireland. This is so if a simple concern for the people who live in Northern Ireland is recognised as valid – structural arguments and more ambitious analyses being left to others. Whatever is understood by the term 'human rights' no one can deny that the citizens of Northern Ireland from all sections of the community, and whatever their political and religious views, have experienced appalling deprivations in recent years. The life-styles, freedoms and privileges taken for granted by individuals in most Western societies have been drastically reduced and curtailed as the violence and political conflict have continued over the last decade. Northern Ireland's 'troubles' constitute a test case for the proper, appropriate and justifiable stances of Governments faced with terrorist challenges but attached to some notion of the rule of law.

The context may be outlined starkly. From 1971 until March

1980 the number of civilians who have died, been killed, as a direct result of the troubles is 1,421. In addition 432 members of the Army and the Ulster Defence Regiment have been killed. 132 members of the Royal Ulster Constabulary have been killed. There have been 28,000 shooting incidents and the number of bomb explosions is over 6,500 – devices which ranged from 5 lbs to over 1,000 lbs of explosives. The number of armed robberies amounts to over 8,400 and, in the last six years alone, there have been nearly 3,000 malicious fires. Estimates of the number of people maimed, incapacitated or seriously injured amount to over 21,000 people. All this of course in a Province with a total population of only 1,500,000 people. It is thus possible, in a morbid way, to calculate how many hours pass before someone is shot, a bomb is planted, an individual is maimed or a gun battle takes place. It is also possible to calculate how many families must have been directly affected through a member of their family being involved, injured or maimed.

There are other statistics. It is said almost 9,000 people have been brought before the courts in the last nine years charged with serious terrorist crimes. These include murder, attempted murder, fire arms and explosives offences. The security forces have searched over 300,000 houses during the troubles – on average 20,000 being searched each year. Under various emergency powers thousands of people have been stopped for questioning, or held in custody. Under the Emergency Provisions Acts of 1973, 1975 and 1978 and the Prevention of Terrorism Act 1976 wide ranging powers to stop, question and arrest were granted to the security forces. It has been alleged that these powers are abused to harass or screen the population. Malpractice in the interrogation of suspects has been alleged by local groups and by Amnesty International. For most of the population it is commonplace to be stopped and questioned about one's identity, ownership of motor car etc. There are random security checks on almost every road. The incidence and intensity of such checks, as with all security measures, oscillates according to policy and the prevailing level of terrorist activity. Yet the 'presence' is continuously and insistently there.

There are sectarian paramilitary forces on both sides – Loyalist and Republican. Some, like the Provisional IRA, the Irish National Liberation Army and the Ulster Volunteer Force are proscribed as illegal organisations. They appear to have the capability to continue to kill and bomb selected targets. In some areas of Belfast and elsewhere in South Armagh there are so-called 'no-go' areas, that is the Police or Army do not maintain control. For individual citizens the restrictions on their mundane activities are manifold. Freedom of movement is cut down by the entrenched divisions in the community which render some routes or journeys inadvisable. Simple tasks like shopping, going to work or seeking entertainment, are made complex by security operations. In many areas motor cars may not be parked – in others only if a passenger remains in the car. Some people, because of their occupation or place of residence, have to take daily precautions before using their cars or opening the front doors of their houses. In the streets armed soldiers scout round vigilant against snipers' attacks. Army Saracen trucks and Land Rovers patrol the towns and villages while police stations are surrounded by high fences, barbed wire, concrete barriers, and pillboxes.

Acts of violence which are relatively spontaneous or sporadic in other countries have become regular and almost customised; there is a continuing dialogue of violence which is virtually institutionalised. In spite of this, and as a monument to human adaptability, life goes on. It is not normal life and should never for a moment be accepted as such, but it goes on.

Meanwhile Northern Irish politicians from both communities (the majority and the minority) offer competing advice on policies and security operations. Direct Rule of Northern Ireland from Westminster continues, although talks with political parties and discussions between Her Majesty's Government and the Taoiseach in the Republic of Ireland are reported in the press. Calls for more, new and further political initiatives emanate regularly from Europe and North America. This is, and for many years has remained, the context for discussions about human rights in Northern Ireland.

During the last decade there have been a series of inquiries and investigations into conditions in Northern Ireland. The Cameron Report, the Hunt Report, the Scarman Report, the Compton Report, the Widgery Report, the Parker Report, the Diplock Report, the Gardiner Report, the Bennett Report . . . all in one way or another suggested ways of tackling the problems that emerge when a democratic government has its legitimacy impugned, when a divided community is polarised, and when groups seek to destroy the government, the legal system and the State itself. An enormous range of political solutions have been mooted. The Sunningdale agreement, the Assembly, the Convention, and numerous variations on the theme of 'powersharing' between Loyalist and Republican parties have been considered. The ingenuity and imagination of constitutional lawyers and theorists, in addition to party politicians, have been tested to the full in the deliberations so far. Direct Rule from Westminster continues *faute de mieux* and the troubles continue. Laws have been passed to combat terrorism and attempt to stamp out violence. The major powers are now enacted in the Emergency Provisions (Northern Ireland) Act 1978 and the Prevention of Terrorism Act 1976. Under the latter, organisations suspected of utilising terrorist violence have been proscribed. Individuals may be expelled from one part of the United Kingdom to another. The powers contained in the former are extensive. Section 12 deals with detention – what used to be called internment without trial. Under Section 7 the trial of scheduled offences (statutory or common law offences usually involving violence *and* committed for terrorist ends) is conducted before a judge sitting alone without a jury – the so-called Diplock Courts. In two other sections of the Act it appears the normal provisions relating to onus of proof (whereby an accused is assumed innocent until proven guilty) have been amended or reversed. Under Sections 11, 13, 14 and 15 members of the security forces have unusual powers to arrest, detain in custody and search premises. Section 8, relating to admissibility of confessions, borrows from the European Convention on Human Rights the phrase that no conduct amounting to 'torture or inhuman or degrading treatment' may be used to elicit a confession.

These extraordinary or minimal provisions have been criticised by various organisations – by the National Council for Civil Liberties, the Peace People, the Northern Ireland Civil Rights Association. The finding by the European Court of Human Rights[1] that the United Kingdom, through the activities of members of the security forces, had been guilty of 'inhuman or degrading treatment' of some persons held in custody, and the publicity given to the Amnesty International Report alleging ill-treatment by the RUC of persons held in custody heightened the concern about the 'emergency powers'. In H-Block prisoners convicted of terrorist offences have 'gone on the blanket' and refuse to wear prison uniform or accept prison rules: the impasse created, and its deeply worrying consequences, attract ghoulish and controversial publicity.

Yet other factors require to be mentioned. While the power to detain without trial exists on the statute book it has not been used since 1975 (even though the European Court of Human Rights viewed the power as justified by the emergency conditions). Parliament passed the Emergency Provisions Acts but only on the basis they should not be permanent – there are periodic renewal debates where the need for continuing each and all the powers are debated. Independent studies have found the Diplock Courts to operate fairly, and many people regard the suspension of jury trial as necessary, if regrettable, because of fear of intimidation of jurors or of potential backlash decisions. The British Government gave an assurance that the practices impeached at the European Court would never be repeated; the Bennett Committee inquired into many aspects of police practice arising from the Amnesty International Report (even if the actual allegations were not fully investigated). Far reaching amendments to the police rules and practices have been introduced.

In areas less overtly concerned with terrorism and emergency powers, there are other significant measures relating to human rights. An Ombudsman was established in 1969 and there is a Commissioner of Complaints who deals with grievances against local councils. The Incitement to Hatred Act 1970 imposed penalties for activities that might incite or promote hatred. A Police Authority was established in 1970 and, to some extent, it can supervise the police force. A Police Complaints Board has been set up. Prosecution of all scheduled offences is only with the consent of the independent Director of Public Prosecutions. There is the Standing Advisory Commission on Human Rights, established in 1973, to advise the Secretary of State for Northern Ireland on the effectiveness of the law in preventing discrimination on grounds of religious belief or political opinion. The Fair Employment Agency was established by statute in 1976 to promote equality of opportunity and provide redress for unlawful discrimination on religious or political grounds. There is an

Equal Opportunities Commission which can investigate unlawful practices involving sexual discrimination.

The activities of the Human Rights Commission are adequately described in its Annual Reports. Despite a technically narrow remit which delimits its powers of inquiry it has been concerned with a wide range of matters – from divorce and homosexuality provisions in Northern Ireland to periods of remand in custody and most of the major powers in the Emergency Provisions Act. It has argued to successive Secretaries of State that some of the specific powers in the Emergency Provisions Act of 1978 should be allowed to lapse – but without success. In 1977 the Advisory Commission published *The Protection of Human Rights by law in Northern Ireland*[2] which is perhaps the most systematic treatment of the role of law in determining and protecting the rights and obligations of individuals where emergency conditions prevail. The Commission called for a Bill of Rights to be introduced and it has repeated this call ever since –participating in and gaining from parallel developments in Britain.

The Commission's reasoning may be briefly summarised. Two important, if seemingly negative, points were emphasised at the outset. First the Commission said it did not under-estimate the scope or effectiveness of the present law in force designed to protect human rights. Second it did not believe or suggest a Bill of Rights would end violence or even significantly affect the level of terrorism. Yet the Commission did see the need for an explicit and general statement of fundamental rights – it diagnosed a need for further protection of human rights. Having considered the arguments against such a course it, like the House of Lords Select Committee in its turn, rejected these arguments. The Standing Advisory Commission found that the majority of those who gave evidence to it favoured a Bill of Rights. Equally they favoured a Bill of Rights for the United Kingdom as a whole and not for Northern Ireland alone ... 'important legal and constitutional considerations ... would make an exclusively Northern Ireland Bill both inappropriate and undesirable'.

The clear statement that there there should be a Bill of Rights for the United Kingdom was based on reasons subsequently rehearsed by proponents of a Bill in Britain. Compliance with international obligations, providing effective legal safeguards against the misuse of power, giving explicit recognition to basic human rights and freedoms, ensuring uniformity throughout the United Kingdom, articulating general principles or criteria to assist legislators, administrators and judges alike, and emphasising the binding values of a democratic society were alluded to. The Commission accepted that Parliament must remain at the centre of constitutional arrangements in the United Kingdom but called for incorporation of the substantive provisions of the European Convention on Human Rights, arguing along the lines now proposed in Lord Wade's Bill to introduce a Bill of Rights. Yet it must also be clear the Commission drew on the experience in Northern Ireland itself during recent years in making its recommendation that there should be a Bill of Rights.

No one with experience of Northern Ireland could plausibly claim that the introduction of a Bill of Rights would be a panacea. Northern Ireland represents uniquely tragic circumstances – pockmarked by outrages, personal grief, sectarian hatred, loss of life . . . in ways which challenge one's credulity. It is the responsibility of those with political, executive and judicial powers to make the decisions which will influence future developments. What the call for a Bill of Rights amounts to – no more or less – is that this must be aided by, and within the framework of, the recognition and protection of fundamental human rights and freedoms. No matter the pressures or exigencies of any particular situation, some values need to be recognised as pre-eminent. The issue of derogation is less important than many think – it is the commitment to fundamental values which is vital. The commitment should come from all those empowered to take decisions – and all others who are not – as constituting an irrebuttable basis for social and political action.

While Bills of Rights have been discussed by academics, the issues involved are not academic. If we are candid we will admit that our understanding of 'human rights' is imperfect and we have barely begun, in complex societies, to clarify the mutual inter-relationships of different freedoms and responsibilities, rights and duties. At the moment the call for the protection of 'human rights' is tantamount to entering a plea for the sort of society we should live in. In the seventeenth and eighteenth centuries where the philosophical pedigree of human rights literature is to be found, the vital matter was to ground a claim for individuals *against* Government. Then recognition of human rights posited a version of society as an association of individuals which was subject to Government but which had rights against Government. In modern welfare states such a theme can appear dreadfully outmoded if not naive. The complexity of industrialised societies and the scope of the welfare state are now such that constraints on individual freedoms which would have appalled those who founded the 'liberal philosophies' in earlier centuries, are not only taken for granted but understood to be vitally important.

In Northern Ireland the Shackleton Report[3] recognised the importance of protecting civil liberties and avoiding interference with individuals' freedoms but said that this must be within the context of recognising an elemental right – the right to live and walk without fear. How the conflicting claims and demands of people holding different political views and social aspirations may best be balanced, presents difficult and agonising decisions for all but the idealogue or the fool. Articulating a Bill of Rights on the basis of the careful models already available would provide relevant parameters. Perhaps no more. A Bill of Rights would not present easy or ready answers but it would allow questions, which may otherwise go by default, to be seriously considered. It would at least be a start in tackling problems where a lot of catching up needs to be done. The introduction of a Bill of Rights might not be sufficient but it is necessary. Northern Ireland has provided that lesson at least.

Emergency Conditions: *Professor Kevin Boyle*

Any discussions about a Bill of Rights would be consigned to irrelevance, if we did not consider the emergency conditions which exist in Northern Ireland because of the campaign of violence. The issues relevant to the Bill of Rights debate have shifted, over this last decade, from the minority's grievances about the local administration, to issues involved in the emergency legal powers which are the direct responsibility of the United Kingdom Government and Parliament.

The concept of an emergency refers to both the occasion for the use of powers, and to the character of the powers themselves. As in the Republic of Ireland and other common law countries, emergency powers may be available to governmental authorities in permanent legislative form. There may or may not be a prescribed procedure for activating these powers – such as the declaration of an emergency as in the Republic of Ireland. Speaking only of powers connected with security, public safety or state security, the additional powers available in an emergency may relate to legislative competence, governmental and administrative authority and the judicial system, as well as to an increase of enforcement powers to the police and military. In the Northern Ireland case, talk of emergency powers is, in effect, about an emergency regime of authority affecting all dimensions of state functions.

It is familiar analysis to note that coercive state powers give rise to two basic issues: efficacy and control. The regulation of power through law must facilitate an effective response to crime (whether ordinary crime or terrorist violence) while simultaneously constraining that response so that it is compatible with democratic values. The problems in maintaining this balance between liberty and security is the central human rights theme in Northern Ireland, as acknowledged by the Standing Advisory Commission on Human Rights.[4] Moreover, it seems likely to remain the central issue. If nothing can be said for a Bill of Rights relevant to the current extreme conditions of public security, then the debate is dead as far as Northern Ireland is concerned.

If the major contributions that a Bill of Rights can make to a democratic political order are thought of as twofold, as a means of stabilising the legal and constitutional order, and as a system of special protection for citizens' rights, then in the Northern Ireland context the case for the irrelevance of a Bill of Rights is not difficult to make. After several brave attempts, the political system remains as fractured as ever. The unanimity with which political groups have endorsed the desirability of a Bill of Rights has only served to highlight their disagreement on other issues, and to emphasise that a Bill of Rights can protect a settlement, but not produce one. Meanwhile, the many human rights reforms introduced in Northern Ireland over this last decade fight a continuing and disheartening battle to achieve results against the fact of political violence and the response to that by the State.

Advocates of a Bill of Rights for the United Kingdom often, by default, make the case against a Bill of Rights because of their assumption that public emergencies which will permit, in their thinking, a derogation from any Bill of Rights are a marginal question. It may look so from London – it does not from Belfast. The European Convention on Human Rights which has been a source of inspiration for the Bill of Rights movement, has had its impact qualified as far as Northern Ireland was concerned since 1957, when derogation affecting the central rights protected in the Convention, personal liberty (Article 5) and due process (Article 6) was entered. That derogation has never been withdrawn. Northern Ireland thus has been excluded over the effective life of the Convention from its major provisions due to 'a public emergency affecting the life of the nation' (Article 15).

However my view is that a Bill of Rights *does* have relevance to the difficult issues raised by public emrgencies. The maintenance of the status quo – with the European Convention as a system of outer protection limited not only by its remoteness from the conflict but by the restrictions placed on it by the effects of derogations combined with the common law system – leaves a human rights vacuum that has itself contributed to the problem of violence in Northern Ireland. That vacuum can be filled, even in the context of an emergency, by an adequate Bill of Rights.

I have moved away from a position I once held that it might be possible to draft a Bill of Rights with such economy that it would be unnecessary to concede power to the authorities to derogate from it whatever the special circumstances. Experience elsewhere in the world indicates that if the conditions of attack on the political order are perceived as serious enough, power will 'jump the traces' of the democratic forms including law, and put at risk all rights and liberties. Provision for derogation acknowledges that risk and attempts to prevent it. On the other hand the world is replete with regimes that have, on the basis of actual or pretended emergencies, set aside rights permanently or have otherwise used emergency powers to undermine rather than protect democratic politics and values. The risk of abuse is inherent in the emergency doctrine. What marks off a democratic political order is not necessarily the nature of the powers used, but rather the safeguards provided for control of the powers.

Reviewing the last decade in Northern Ireland, I do not think that one can say that the legal system was prepared for the task of responding to the violence, or, in particular, of providing safeguards against the abuse of executive authority. Nothing more eloquently makes the case for a Bill of Rights than the weary history of the response to terrorism in Northern Ireland. The availability of a Bill of Rights in previous years, prior to the violence, allowing access to the courts and the airing of grievances, might well have meant that we would not have experienced the intensity, duration and scale of conflict that we now witness. Looking at the peripheral role of law and lawyers in the history of Northern Ireland in the context of the protection of human rights, it would, it seems to me, be a brave man who would still praise the virtues of an unwritten constitution.

The arguments in favour of a Bill of Rights as part of the framework of the legal system in emergency conditions are several. First, the existence of the Bill of Rights would supply standards and principles relevant to the assessment of the use of emergency powers and to the supervision of powers. Second, the Bill of Rights would make the issue of the justification for powers, and their exercise, a more central preoccupation of legal procedures. Third, while human rights are increasingly thought of as indivisible, the concept of fundamental rights, including the right to life and freedom from torture, which must be afforded the same respect and protection in an emergency as in normal times, has clearly great importance in an emergency. Fourth, a Bill of Rights as part of the fundamental domestic law of the state which emphasises the responsibility of the state for the protection of human rights and its commitment to that protection, must be especially significant where the state itself is under attack and is liable to panic. Fifth, the existence of a fundamental statement of rights combined with human rights education would help to sensitise the legal profession to the vulnerability of individuals' rights under emergency conditions. Finally, all of these points are reinforced by having regard to the specific features of the Northern Ireland emergency, the duration of the violence and the divided community which endures its impact. Whatever force these points in favour of a Bill of Rights have, they rest on one pivotal assumption. It is that in an emergency the authorities responding to it *are* accountable; that, notwithstanding special powers, the compatibility of those powers and their exercise with the fundamental law, may be raised.

Yet I must express strong disagreement with the Standing Advisory Commission's view on a Bill of Rights. The Commission suggests that the authorities exercising emergency powers should be accountable only to Parliament for the decision to use the emergency powers that would derogate from a Bill of Rights, and as to the proportionality of measures taken under these powers. That, I submit, is fundamentally wrong headed: it is throwing the baby out with the bath-water. It is bluntly common law thinking: it represents a return to the position described by Lord Scarman of 'black and white: you either have a peaceable society in which rights are protected or you have untrammelled power with all rights at risk or set at nought'. Rather I argue that it is a hallmark of a democratic system's response to an emergency that the authorities are prepared to account for a resort to emergency before independent judicial and/or other authorities. This is a central concept in the European Convention on Human Rights and other major international instruments. It should equally be central as far as a Bill of Rights in the Northern Ireland context is concerned.

Looking back over the last decade can one express confidence in the untrammelled political process in Parliament as a means of ensuring a balanced response to terrorism? The decade is studded with the overthrow of fundamental constitutional legal decisions, and reveals a deliberate policy of marginalising the role of the judiciary in the review of the exercise of emergency powers. Yet though the domestic courts are denied a supervisory role the government is accountable in law for the quality and proportionality of its response to the emergency at the international level. It is unacceptable that this should be so. The Strasbourg machinery, particularly in an emergency, does not provide an adequate system for monitoring emergency powers nor of affording redress. The parliamentary and administrative processes are plainly inadequate in dealing with an ongoing emergency.

Two current examples illustrate this point vividly. If one looks at the way the H-Block question has been allowed to persist and develop to its present desperate state, one must surely question whether the embattled administration has in any sense had its actions subject to supervision or scrutiny. The value of independent scrutiny is that at least the whole case emerges. (That, by the way, would not necessarily be to the advantage of the prisoners.) But no one can claim that what was been happening in the H-Blocks has been fully revealed. The Government has concealed matters and has resorted to propaganda in the sense of emphasising the questions and issues which put its position in the best light. There ought now, in my view, as an interim measure, to be an immediate independent judicial inquiry into the circumstances at the Maze Prison. Similar dissatisfaction with the career of the interrogation controversy has been expressed by the Standing Advisory Commission.[5] It is unsatisfactory to allow allegations about ill-treatment to fester until they erupt into a controversy which demands an inquiry. Much unnecessary damage to confidence in law and its administration has been done by the way in which these issues have been handled. In my opinion both illustrate institutional failures in the legal system.

I am therefore arguing for the maintenance of judicial supervision in the context of an emergency. Let it not be said against the case for such supervision that one is reluctant to give such a task to the Northern Ireland judiciary. The extraordinary achievement of the judiciary in Northern Ireland over this decade of political conflict and violence is a matter for record. If the courts, in the past, appeared indifferent or insensitive to questions of human rights it was no more than the insensitivity reflected at legislative and governmental levels. The courts at least had the excuse that the narrow jurisdiction granted them by our legal system left little opportunity to develop a role in the protection of human rights. But anyone examining the record of the last decade must endorse the view that the courts have given the common law a reputation, more than it probably deserves, in their concern to stand between the citizen and the state in the application of emergency powers. In a recent case *Farrell v. The Ministry of Defence*[6] the Lord Chief Justice recounted counsels' argument that the court should not subject decisions as to military operations to judicial scrutiny because it might mean, for example, looking as far afield as Germany and the army of the Rhine. The Chief Justice replied, essentially, that he did not see this as a problem. That, I submit, is precisely the right constitutional attitude and one that the people in the community want to hear.

The insistence on judicial supervision does not mean that additional mechanisms are unnecessary. Having disagreed with the Standing Advisory Commission on some specific points let me end by agreeing with their arguments and proposals concerning the control of emergency powers. As the Commission say, *there is a need* for a monitoring agency in Northern Ireland with competence to investigate and respond to complaints, and examine patterns of use of powers. In my view there is also need for greater control at Parliamentary level of powers granted in emergency legislation. A Standing Committee on emergency powers should be constituted to monitor policy in the application of such powers. Such a committee should concern itself with the patterns of abuse which might emerge, and be empowered to take action to reverse such patterns. But let us not try to remove the role of our courts in constitutional protection at the very time when the law should not be silent.

A Charter for Northern Ireland: *Terry Carlin*

The policy on a Bill of Rights of the Northern Ireland Committee of the Irish Congress of Trades Unions (ICTU) has been consistent. The statements calling for a Bill of Rights for Northern Ireland range from the publication of *Citizens' Rights in Northern Ireland* (1967) to more recent comments on community and political affairs in 1979. And the demand for a Bill of Rights for Northern Ireland has been re-echoed both at Northern Ireland Annual Conferences, at Annual Conferences of ICTU, and also at the British Trades Union Congress.

In pursuit of this policy, our representatives met the Standing Advisory Commission during the course of its deliberations on *The Protection of Human Rights by Law in Northern Ireland.*[7] An outside observer at these meetings and others held since the Commission's Report was published, might have assumed that the strenuous debate between us indicated that the two bodies were poles apart. This is not the case, I am pleased to say. There is agreement on the truly vital issue, that is the need to provide a legal framework for the protection of human rights. The Northern Ireland Committee and the Commission subsequently differ on other matters but before describing our differences in detail, I would like to refer to one or two aspects which are of general relevance as a background to this debate.

In its Report, the Commission stated that 'violence is the greatest single barrier to social and economic advancement, job creation and to inter-community trust ... The violence of the last eight years has steadily reduced the quality of life'.[8] And again 'the continuing state of emergency has not only seriously marred the effectiveness of the substantial legislative and administrative reforms which have been made since 1969 for the better protection of human rights, but has also inevitably resulted in the restrictions of certain basic rights and protections in Northern Ireland'. I concur totally with the Commission's view. Violence is a direct threat to all forms of protection of human rights. It threatens the very right to life which is the most basic, fundamental human right; it threatens other rights such as the right to a home, the right to employment. Many of our people have lost these rights due to acts of violence.

The Northern Ireland Committee also accepts the view of the Commission that a Bill of Rights in itself will not end the violence in Northern Ireland. Unfortunately, in the past there has been a tendency to regard the better protection of human rights as being irrelevant or totally inappropriate in a situation of continuing violence. We certainly agree that there must be political, economic, social and security provisions which provide for the safety and liberty of all the citizens of Northern Ireland. The question therefore arises whether there is any merit in codifying citizens' rights in a Bill or Charter of Rights, given the violence continues and granted that there has been a substantial body of legislation enacted over the last decade for the protection of rights.

My view and that of the Northern Ireland Committee of ICTU is that if you could provide that the 20 most important human rights were protected by 20 seperate pieces of legislation backed up by a battery of subsidiary Orders and Regulations, we would *still* wish to see a Bill of Rights which collated and codified those rights. We feel that a Bill or Charter of Rights has a moral superiority over a mere legislative Act, even if that Act itself confers rights to the citizens.

One of the problems obviously is the problem of the lack of a written constitution for the UK as a whole. But the absence of that written constitution is increasingly less of an issue in this discussion. More and more frequently, issues which arise within the United Kingdom end up at the international tribunals at Strasbourg or Luxembourg. We have had cases which have emanated from Northern Ireland. A totally non-contentious example is provided by the pig farmers in Northern Ireland who challenged the validity of the operations of the Pig Marketing Board under the Treaty of Rome of the European Economic Community. One might be tempted to say that if the pigs of Northern Ireland can take the Government to Court, then the people should have the same rights! Less facetiously we contend that a framework of rights should be such as to be enforceable in *both* the domestic and international courts, so that individuals do not have to wait for inordinate periods of time to have their cases considered, as currently happens in raising cases before international tribunals.

The question of the status of a Bill of Rights has been much discussed. The Northern Ireland Committee considered whether or not a Bill of Rights should be enacted in a straightforward manner by statute or whether it should be *entrenched* or require a special majority at the Westminster Parliament. We believe that the enactment of a Bill of Rights by the normal Parliamentary processes would be sufficient, because it would appear in the eyes of both our own people and the outside world to have a status over and above that of any other, 'ordinary' Act of Parliament. This would simply be because it *was* a Bill of Rights. Governments, of whatever complexion, would be reluctant to water down or remove rights contained in a Charter or a Bill of Rights, knowing that any such moves would be seen in the international community as being retrospective and reactionary. The Bill could of course also be afforded special status by containing a clause that all previous and subsequent legislation must concur with the provisions of the Bill of Rights, except insofar as an *express* declaration to the contrary was contained in a subsequent Act of Parliament. This would however entail very radical extensions to some of the normal legislative processes.

In all the matters referred to so far, the Northern Ireland Committee and the Human Rights Commission are more or less of the same mind. The Commission however (with the exception of Mr Cooper in his Note of Dissent) believed that a Bill of Rights for the United Kingdom as a whole is the proper solution. The Northern Ireland Committee does not see any real political possibility of such a Bill being introduced for the United Kingdom as a whole in the foreseeable future. We know of course about the progress made by Lord Wade's Bill and have read reports concerning the possibility of an all-Party conference being convened: these and other developments might seem to indicate the prospects of a Bill of Rights for the United Kingdom being introduced are improving. But any realistic analysis shows the progress made has been very limited indeed and none of the major hurdles has yet been cleared.

We believe that it would be right, proper and feasible to introduce a Bill of Rights for Northern Ireland. If, as with some of the current emergency legislation, it is possible to treat the rights of citizens of Northern Ireland as being rights which they hold distinct from rights they hold as citizens of the United Kingdom, then it must be possible to reverse the process. Although I have lived and worked most of my life within the United Kingdom, I can be expelled from Britain and made to return to Northern Ireland. This is so because of legislation made in Westminster. My rights within a very substantial proportion of the United Kingdom can be restricted by a Deportation Order from the Home Secretary. Rights as citizens of Northern Ireland and as citizens of the United Kingdom are not therefore exactly coterminous. Similarly provisions can and should be introduced which will protect rights in Northern Ireland, in ways which need not apply in the rest of the United Kingdom.

Such a course, of introducing a Bill of Rights in Northern Ireland, could be relevant to the debate in Britain. A Bill of Rights introduced in Northern Ireland, as a matter of urgency, could allow for further consideration and give some practical experience which could be taken into account in the wider debate relating to the United Kingdom as a whole.

Finally the Northern Ireland Committee holds firmly to the view that the introduction of a Bill of Rights for Northern Ireland should *not* be part of any political horse-trading between political parties. It should be introduced to back any agreement or proposals which may emerge from either the political parties of Northern Ireland, or the Westminster Government irrespective of what else those proposals or agreements may contain.

If a Bill of Rights is the proper course forward, then it should be introduced and introduced at an early date.

Legal Rights and Political Control: *Lord Melchett*

Lord Scarman has asked whether anyone seriously considers

that there is no need to reform our law insofar as it concerns the protection of human rights. Of course such a need exists; but to answer that question in the affirmative is not the same as saying the the *best* way of reforming our law is by enacting a Bill of Rights. I do not believe it is. Let me make a couple of prefatory points which may help place arguments which have not received sufficient attention in context.

It would, as others have remarked, be thoroughly naive to suppose that the present Tory Government, or the sort of consensus in the House of Lords that supported Lord Wade's Bill, is going to agree to any Bill of Rights that threatened to affect, in any significant way, any provisions contained in the emergency legislation currently in force in Northern Ireland or Great Britain. This is worth bearing in mind.

Also I agree with Lord Boston that incorporation of the European Convention on Human Rights would introduce great uncertainties into, and uncertainty about, the state of our law. It is not the uncertainty itself which worries me however – what I am concerned about is who would have power as a result of the uncertainty. The vagueness of the law would result in greatly increased scope for judges to make new law. And the judges would usually be making *political* and *administrative* decisions.

For example, judges would have to decide on the balance between the right of a group of people to defend their right to work for a fair wage in acceptable conditions by banding together (in a closed shop) against the right of an individual *not* to be bound by the majority, or even otherwise unanimous, decision of his or her fellow workers. To take another example, they would have to make judgments about the extent to which the right of parents to decide how their children should be educated could be weighed against the administrative impossibility of providing public funds to every group of parents which wished to run their own school. Similarly the right of parents might have to be balanced against the political view that equality of opportunity demands a universal (though not uniform) system of education.

I do not want to see judges taking more political decisions in our society. More than anything else this is because I do not think that, in any way, they represent the range of political views in our society – either in Britain or in Northern Ireland. My view is that *on the whole* the legal profession is conservative in outlook, and this applies to a greater extent to those lawyers from whom judges are selected. Judges taking political decisions would tend to come down on the side of individual rather than collective rights – and this much more so than would a democratically elected group. I believe that the legal systems in Western capitalist countries are based on a belief that individual rights (such as the right to own private property) are more important that the rights of groups of people. The history of trades union law in Great Britain provides a clear demonstration of this point. Democratically elected Parliaments passed successive Bills to allow workers to organise and join together in unions, to strike, to picket ... and time after time judges reached decisions that reduced or negated the effect of the legislation.

The United States is often quoted as an illustration of the system we should aim for. But those who cite America as a model, as Lord Scarman does, fail to go on to describe the totally different constitutional and legal arrangements that prevail in that country. The United States has politically appointed judges and judges who are *elected* in various ways: judges can be clearly politically labelled and like politicians are known to be Left Wing, Right Wing or whatever. The *political* balance of the Supreme Court is known, and may be altered deliberately by politicians as and when the opportunity arises.

If we only introduced a Bill of Rights *after* we had introduced democratic elections for judges I would have less worries about the proposals. Yet I would *still* have grave doubts about using the *legal* system (as opposed to the political system of local, regional and central government) to achieve improvements in human rights for various reasons.

First, as mentioned, I think the legal system is a system that favours action by individuals and is in favour of individuals as compared with or opposed to groups and group action. Second, I believe that the legal system is designed and/or operates in a way that is seen as intimidating, alien and hostile to the mass of people. Courts are the last place, and lawyers often the last people, that members of the working class would go to for help or redress. It is no accident that there has been such a growth in establishing more informal sources of advice and more informal tribunals. We should be trying to change the law (both criminal and civil) to help people keep away from courts and from

lawyers. Third, it is quite likely that the availability of some
redress for injustice through the courts (an advantage claimed by
the proponents of a Bill of Rights) would encourage the political
system to avoid dealing with 'sensitive' or controversial issues.
For example, the fact that a case about the law on homosexuality
in Northern Ireland has been taken to Strasbourg – and now lies
somewhere between the European Commission and the European Court of Human Rights – has almost certainly allowed the
present Government to sit back and avoid the issue. It is allowed
simply to leave the matter to the Court – changing the law in due
course if it is forced to by the Court – rather than facing the
reactionary opposition to law reform head on.

These last points obviously are related. The fourth reason for
being sceptical about the desirability of introducing a Bill of
Rights rests on different grounds. I think that most *progress* in
protecting and *advancing* human rights has been made through
specific legislation aimed at specific abuses and establishing
enforcement agencies – for example the Equal Opportunities
Commission, the Fair Employment Agency, and the Commission for Racial Equality. Such agencies can not only assist in
enforcing the legislation, but can undertake the necessary
research and other work that may lead to effective pressure for
the desperately needed further advances. This might be more
resources, strengthening of specific legislative measures, and
further enhancing the remit and powers of the agencies concerned with human rights and combating discrimination. (Given
that the present Tory Government seems intent on weakening
such bodies, the point is not a trivial one.)

Fifth, I fear that the debate about a Bill of Rights, and even
worse the passing of such a Bill, would deflect and possibly
swamp the strong campaigns on specific issues that do have some
chance of being effective. For example, everyone who has
considered the matter is agreed that a Bill of Rights has no chance
of affecting the existing emergency legislation in Northern
Ireland or Britain. If that is the case – and it is – should we not
now be concentrating on the sort of proposals that Boyle,
Hadden and Hillyard[9] have made for specific and much needed
changes in the legislation and in Army and Police practice?

The final point allows me to return to both my beginning and to
two particular points made by Lord Scarman. Section 8 of the

Emergency Provisions Act 1978 governs the admissibility of statements made by people in custody in Northern Ireland. Lord Scarman suggested that the judges have limited the effect of this section (although he phrased it more delicately). But the Amnesty International Report stated, and other observers and researchers have suggested, that judges diverge greatly in the way they interpret this section. There can be variance from case to case. What is wrong is section 8 itself, and it is this section that should be repealed. Lord Scarman said the section had led to confusion because it was a piecemeal incorporation of part of the European Convention on Human Rights into the domestic law of Northern Ireland. The solution is simple – repeal the section. Second, Lord Scarman suggested that the opposition in Parliament to Lord Wade's Bill came from the House that is dominated by political parties. I would describe the position differently. The fact is that the unelected, appointed or hereditary, overwhelmingly Conservative (and more overwhelmingly conservative) House of Lords has a majority in favour of Lord Wade's Bill. The democratically elected Chamber, the House of Commons, is a lot less sure.

Defending Civil Liberties: *Patricia Hewitt*

The National Council for Civil Liberties is in favour of incorporating the European Convention on Human Rights into the law throughout the United Kingdom. We are in favour of strengthening the Convention both by borrowing new sections from the United Nations Civil and Political Rights Covenant, and by ratifying Protocol 4 of the European Convention which deals with citizenship and which has never been accepted by the United Kingdom Government. But let me also say that we are quite convinced that incorporation, even of a strengthened Convention far less the Convention in its present form, would in no sense transform the state of civil liberties in the United Kingdom – or in any part of the United Kingdom.

Imagine that a European Convention Act, effecting the incorporation of the Convention, was passed tomorrow. That would not necessarily, depending on how it was drafted, end the existence of the power to intern in Northern Ireland; it would not mean the restoration of the right to trial by jury; it would not in any way strengthen the right of a suspect to receive bail. It would not create an Ombudsman with the power to go into the prisons or interrogation centres; it would not end the system of compulsory prison work or the wearing of prison uniforms. Such an Act would do something. It would, I think, extend homosexual law reform to Northern Ireland; it would give us a basis, not only in Northern Ireland but in Britain as well, for laws to protect individual privacy more effective than those already in existence.

Yet there is a problem here. It is that in Northern Ireland the 'concept' of a Bill of Rights has become a potent symbol in the desire to restore, or rather to create, normal civil and political rights. There is no doubt that the introduction of something called a Bill of Rights or a Charter of Rights would have a very profound psychological effect. The question would remain however whether it would deliver the goods. The answer to that question depends on two contingencies. First of all the political will of the Government and of Parliament at Westminster to respect and retain fundamental standards for recognising and protecting human rights in emergency conditions. If the Government and Parliament continue in their adamant refusal to amend in any serious way, or to repeal, emergency provisions, it is wishful thinking to believe that they are likely to introduce a Bill of Rights that will do precisely what they have consistently refused to do. Indeed since the United Kingdom Government has also refused to extend homosexual law reform to Northern Ireland, it may be a little over-optimistic to think that they are going to accept incorporation of the European Convention which would force them to do something else they have turned their face against.

The second problem relates to the method by which the European Convention is incorporated. With all respect to Lord Wade I am not happy with the formula proposed in his Bill. If Lord Wade's Bill of Rights, as I read it, had been in effect from the beginning of this year its provisions would not have affected the new immigration rules that were introduced in March and which, it has been rightly said, do in certain respects violate the European Convention on Human Rights. Under the Bill as drafted the courts have been left powerless. Similarly they would be powerless if, after passage of Lord Wade's Bill of Rights, Parliament re-enacted the exclusion and detention powers of the Prevention of Terrorism Act 1976. Simply because *those* powers (which we would argue violate the Convention) cannot possibly be interpreted as being consistent with the Convention then, under Lord Wade's Bill, the Convention falls to one side and those powers continue regardless of the violation. This is the effect of Clause 3 of his Bill. Real protection for civil liberties would be much greater if the alternative wording recommended by the Cobden Trust were adopted:

> Any Act passed after this Act shall be so construed and applied as not to abrogate, abridge or infringe or to require, authorise or permit any abrogation, abridgement or infringement of any rights or freedoms mentioned in the Bill of Rights ... insofar as an Act passed after this Act, or any part of such an Act, is incapable of such construction or application as may be required by (the above), it shall not have effect.

As compared with other instruments concerned with civil liberties the European Convention provides only relatively low standards for the protection of human rights. Of course the United Kingdom has been found wanting on a number of occasions – for example in the cases relating to contempt, prisoner's access to a solicitor, treatment of would-be immigrants and, most likely, the laws concerning homosexuals in Northern Ireland. As compared with the Bill of Rights in the United States, for example, the European Convention fails to make positive commitments in a number of significant areas. Equally its inclusion of saving clauses (references to 'national security', 'public order, health or morals etc.') could allow infringement of human rights to be justified by a Government ... when they are not justifiable.

It is thus important to recognise that incorporation of the European Convention would be a modest measure and there is a strong need for continuing political pressure to introduce the law reforms that are necessary. Thus the abolition of the power to intern without trial, the restoration of jury trial and of the normal rules on admissibility of confessions are required in Northern Ireland. There is a danger that without pressure from lawyers and other groups some of these emergency measures may become permanent or become 'the norm'. We have seen tampering with the normal safeguards provided in the administration of justice such that it would be unsurprising if confidence in the legal system was diminished. There is a fear that the rules relating to the admissibility of confessions could provide an inducement to interrogators to gain confessions by the use of improper pressures. Surely current practices should be closely monitored and surely there should be strong and effective bodies to over-view the protection of human rights? The Standing Advisory Commission's statutory remit, and its functions, need to be strengthened.

Therefore we may say that incorporation of the Convention is desirable. It will provide a speedier remedy than is possible in taking cases to Strasbourg; it will provide a badly needed check in the courts against the abuses of power by Parliament. But it is in no sense a panacea and in no sense a substitute for the very painstaking and difficult job which has to be done in Northern Ireland (and I think in Britain) in seeking to introduce the comprehensive, substantive reforms in the manifold areas of law which cry out for reform.

Problems and Prospects: *Brian Garrett*

My two purposes are to attempt to explain the immediacy of discussions about the protection of human rights and to place them in focus, and to suggest – by way of a rough and ready score sheet – what progress has been made recently in Northern Ireland.

Not long ago the inter-Party constitutional talks convened by the Secretary of State for Northern Ireland were adjourned. What may now transpire is a matter for conjecture, but we may well be about to witness an upsurge of public interest (and perhaps acrimonious debate if we are not careful) in arguments about the adequacy of any *written laws* in protecting individuals and groups in the absence of a general political consensus. The debate about a Bill of Rights thus has great relevance to the current situation in Northern Ireland. It is not, and should not become, an academic exercise nor a debate confined to elitist groupings and divorced from the wider context and unrelated to the people most affected. I stress this because, unfortunately, some of the discussions so far have tended to overlook the current political relevance of the subject in hand. In its Report *The Protection of Human Rights by Law in Northern Ireland,*[10] the Standing Advisory Commission posed two questions:

1 Was it desirable to increase the legal protection of human rights in Northern Ireland by a Bill of Rights or otherwise?
2 Should any change be confined to Northern Ireland or should it apply to the United Kingdom as a whole?
In returning to these questions which remain of central importance – and at some risk of appearing self-congratulatory since I was a signatory to the Report – I remain convinced the Commission got the right answers in 1977 and the approach which was adopted remains valid today. We realised that the two questions could not be considered in the abstract, and they could not be answered by some mere 'totting up' of alternative arguments, or by the application of pure logic. In other words we accepted that there was no certain truth, no demonstrable right or wrong that would provide answers. Yet, as the Report says, even if the complex issues demand delicate judgments, that does not justify side-stepping the questions or failing to give reasons for any answers which might be offered.

All of us on the Commission then were very conscious of the need to tackle the questions realistically. Put more directly within the Northern Ireland context this *does* mean taking account of the emergency situation and the continuing violence, and having respect for the strength and character of prevailing opinion. These points should remain constantly before us. It might be tempting to discuss human rights questions as if there were no violence, or some virtually absolute individual freedoms were attainable, but to proceed in this way is to deceive ourselves – more to the point, perhaps, the prospects for any change would be diminished since the public will not be so readily fooled if reform is pursued on such an impracticable basis.

The Commission answered the questions it had posed by suggesting(1) that human rights could and should be strengthened by the introduction of a Bill of Rights in the form of the European Convention on Human Rights and (2) such a Bill of Rights should have application to the whole of the United Kingdom – the defects of a Bill of Rights limited to Northern Ireland being compounded while Direct Rule continued.

There is a growing feeling that the British Government will, before long, make proposals to reintroduce some measure of devolution for Northern Ireland (a move which, incidentally, may well be premature). In view of this one of the less publicised findings of the Commission is relevant today. We said:

> We believe that in the event of the return of devolved legislative and executive functions to a new Government in Northern Ireland ... it would be desirable for the enabling legislation to include a clear and enforceable Charter of rights for Northern Ireland ... this Charter of rights could be more comprehensive than the European Convention and should be framed in the light of whatever at the time seem to be the special needs of the people of Northern Ireland.[11]

Yet whether it is an overall measure for the United Kingdom, or a tailor-made Charter of rights for Northern Ireland in a new devolutionary context, the problem of violence remains and must be faced. The issue of the impact of violence on any human rights reforms cannot be ducked – it is crucial because as the Gardiner Committee[12] noted there is a double perspective in tackling human rights viz. (a) the need to act effectively against those engaged in violence and (b) the importance of ensuring basic rights (and this means basic rights though not necessarily all adjectival rights and practices) for those who are brought before the courts notwithstanding the gravity of the charge or the sense of public outrage which may exist.

I am bound to state, with all the force I can, that I do not believe *any* human rights reforms are likely to have an effect on the attitudes of those perpetrating the violence in Northern Ireland today. Twelve years of violence tells me those responsible are not interested in reform, and that it is proper for the Government to act with determination against those engaged in such illegal conspiracies. But to admit this does not mean that reforms would have no effect at all – far from it. It might well be that reforms, where justified, will be able in the medium term to strike at the roots of community discontent on which, for example, the IRA is so heavily dependent and on which it feeds. Nonetheless we must not aim for reforms simply for reform's sake – acting in some social vacuum and unrelated to identifiable and desired social objectives. I am then convinced the Commission got it right in 1977 in suggesting the incorporation of the European Convention into United Kingdom law and that view holds good today particularly if it is allied to the other detailed measures suggested in the Report. I am not convinced the impact in Northern Ireland would be as great as some might hope it might be; and it remains my belief that a substantial measure of derogation from the terms of the Convention would be necessary as far as Northern Ireland is concerned. It is in reviewing our other proposal – that a Charter of rights should accompany a new devolutionary experiment – that I find I have greater doubts.

It is not that such rights would not be desirable (whatever the form of devolution) but rather, in my view, the present deadlock between the main political parties might suggest the notion that there is some written constitution (including 'Bill of Rights provisions') which is a substitute for political consensus or a guarantee of a reasonable degree of inter-community confidence. Such ideas are surely fallacious in Northern Ireland where the very legitimacy of the state is central to the political debate. This may seem an unduly pessimistic viewpoint but I do not believe it to be so. If I am correct, and such a Charter of rights is to be promulgated, it is for us to demonstrate the likely implications of such rights within the overall political context so that the general public may be able to assess the issues accurately. Also by acknowledging whatever limitations do exist so far as purely *written* laws are concerned, one will identify at the same time the *strengths* which such laws would also be likely to possess.

Senator Robinson has discussed human rights in the Republic of Ireland and this gave considerable insight into the activities of the judges in that jurisdiction. Yet it suggested to me that there might be a dangerous confusion of form and substance – a confusion which is present in Northern Ireland as well. We may agree there has been worthwhile judicial work in the Republic of Ireland, particularly in the field of family law, but that still leaves the question why that work is necessary. The firm answer to that important question is 'Because in Ireland a socially monolithic and sectarian constitution has attacked individual liberty'. Thus it is correct to say to the judges 'well done' but then to say to the politicians 'you, not the judges, are those most able to do something really worthwhile in changing the setting in which such abuses occur'. If I am right we should take note of the same point for Northern Ireland.

Finally, and only very briefly, I wish to glance at the score-sheet of human rights in Northern Ireland which I mentioned at the outset. Not surprisingly there is something of a mixed bag. Yet it may allow some summary of the main features of human rights in Northern Ireland today, as compared with 1977 when the Commission published its Report. Some of the features can only be regarded as minuses but there are others on the plus side.

The minuses that have to be mentioned include
- the continuing violence
- the failure of the criminal law enforcement legislation concerning extra-territorial crimes
- the failure to reform the law on homosexual practices to bring it into line with the rest of the United Kingdom, and the avoidance of any debate about abortion law reform
- the effect of the decline in the economy; I recognize I thus mix economic values and legal issues but they have a relationship affecting opportunities of citizens
- the continuing problems and doubts over admissibility of evidence in courts.

There are other features, however, on the plus side:

- the major achievements made under the Fair Employment legislation, undoubtedly the most noteworthy success over the entire decade
- the apparent increasing use of legal processes in a juris diction where, it has been argued, in the past the majority had little confidence in the Northern Ireland judiciary
- the substantial evidence of the existence of a vigorous and independently minded judiciary at work in Northern Ireland
- the beneficial effect of approved legal aid provisions
- the fact that the emergency legislation is kept under review
- the existence of the Equal Opportunities legislation
- the role and influence of the bodies in Strasbourg concerned with the European Convention on Human Rights
- above all else an increasing realisation and acceptance that terrorism cannot win and must be defeated.

The score sheet is unsatisfactory. But the plus side does outweigh the minuses. This is against all the odds and in defiance of the bomb and the bullets.

Part III

THE EUROPEAN CONVENTION AND THE EUROPEAN COMMUNITY

Earlier chapters in this book have discussed the key issues in considering a Bill of Rights in the United Kingdom and the special urgencies and difficulties created by violence and terrorism. But the focus of the debate remains on the incorporation into domestic law of the European Convention on Human Rights. The Convention is admired as a Charter, its introduction would enhance uniformity and harmonisation with other Western European countries. Yet the Convention is not a static document and other important European developments, which may affect the United Kingdom, are emerging.

John Smythe outlines the operation of the European Commission and the European Court of Human Rights and describes the demands and prospects for further enhancement and development of the Convention itself. The Convention has been flexible – other changes are under way. Dr Claus-Dieter Ehlermann describes the important and ambitious announcement by the Commission of the EEC that the Community itself should accede to the European Convention. Such a development could profoundly affect the law in the United Kingdom. Professor J. E. S. Fawcett, President of the European Commission of Human Rights, poses fundamental questions about a Bill for the United Kingdom. Touching on the European Convention as drafted, he ranges more widely over examples from other countries to explore the alternatives that should be further considered if there is to be a Bill of Rights for the United Kingdom.

THE EUROPEAN CONVENTION IN OPERATION

John Smythe

By way of introduction it is well perhaps to recall that the European Convention on Human Rights was signed in November 1950. To date it has been ratified by twenty out of the twenty-one member states of the Council of Europe. The Convention constitutes a collective guarantee at international European level of a number of basic principles and provides special judicial machinery to uphold them. Three international bodies form this machinery. They are:

1 the European Commission of Human Rights
2 the European Court of Human Rights
3 the Committee of Ministers of the Council of Europe.

The European Commission consists of a number of members equal to the number of Contracting States. Its members are elected for six years by the Committee of Ministers from a list of names drawn up by the Bureau of the Parliamentary Assembly of the Council of Europe. The members are in practice selected on the basis of one from each Contracting State; they sit in their individual capacity which ensures genuine independence. The Commission may receive complaints against States from another contracting State (Article 24) or, subject to the State in question having recognised what is known as the right of individual petition (Article 25) from private persons or non-governmental organisations (see Table p. 113).

The Commission's first task is to decide whether a complaint merits full investigation – this is termed the admissibility stage. Where an application discloses no indication of a sustainable grievance under the Convention, it may be dismissed by the Commission without even being brought to the notice of the State in question. When a case is admitted, the Commission proceeds to carry out an inquiry, and seeks to bring about a friendly settlement. Should no settlement be reached, the Commission draws up a report stating its opinion as to whether there is a breach of the Convention.

The European Court comprises as many judges as there are member States of the Council of Europe. The judges are elected by the Parliamentary Assembly and are independent. Subject to Contracting States to the Convention having by optional declaration (Article 46) accepted its competence, the European Court of Human Rights has jurisdiction to take a final and binding decision which may include awarding compensation. The Commission or a State, but not an individual complainant, can bring a case before the Court. If a case is not so referred, it is decided by the Committee of Ministers of the Council of Europe by a two-thirds majority, and the Committee prescribes, where appropriate, a period for taking measures to remedy matters.

These three bodies, the European Commission and Court of Human Rights and the Committee of Ministers of the Council of Europe, all with headquarters at Strasbourg, are, of course, quite distinct and separate from the similarly named institutions of the European Communities where there are a Commission and a Council of Ministers at Brussels and the European Court of Justice at Luxembourg.

It would be out of place here to attempt to review the history of the European Convention over the past three decades. The very brief outline given above of how the Treaty operates is, I trust, sufficient as a basis to concentrate on new horizons, to see in what directions the Convention may be going in the eighties, stressing certain features which could have a direct bearing on its future course.

The first topic I would like to mention is the substantive content of the Convention, that is the scope and character of the rights and freedoms which are protected. These are essentially traditional or classical freedoms and the obligation on the Contracting State is, broadly speaking, to forebear from doing anything infringing their enjoyment. In recent years, however, there has been a growing body of opinion which considers that basic rights cannot be limited to the traditional freedoms. Rather it is thought the catalogue should and could be extended to include what are known as 'social and economic rights' – rights relating to employment, a right to social security benefits and such like. The argument generally runs . . . what use is it to man to know he cannot be imprisoned save by sentence of a court when he may be hungry and ill-housed? The pressure generated within States by this body of opinion is strengthened in international circles by freely-voiced criticism from Third World countries of the Western European States for their tendency, as it is said, to stick to traditional viewpoints and concentrate on luxuries such as parliamentary democray with all its niceties of behaviour. One thus finds the debate going on at two levels and there are some indications that the industrialised West would wish to find some way of meeting the criticism. In short, the question arises whether the so-called social and economic rights should and could be written into the Convention and made subject to the specific complaints procedure set up by the Convention. These are certainly matters to be discussed when one considers what the term 'human rights' must cover in a Bill of Rights or an International Convention.

In the context of the Convention as it stands I would like to draw your attention to a passage from the judgment of the European Court of Human Rights in the case of Mrs Airey concerning the Republic of Ireland. The Government's final submission was that 'the Convention should not be interpreted so as to achieve social and economic developments in a Contracting State; such developments can only be progressive.' In dealing with this point the judgment reads as follows:

> The Court is aware that the further realisation of social and economic rights is largely dependent on the situation – notably financial – reigning in the State in question. On the other hand, the Convention must be interpreted in the light of present-day conditions and it is designed to safeguard the individual in a real and practical way as regards those areas with which it deals. Whilst the Convention sets forth what are essentially civil and political rights, many of them have implications of a social or economic nature. The Court therefore considers, like the Commission, that the mere fact that an interpretation of the Convention may extend into the sphere of social and economic rights should not be a decisive factor against such an interpretation; there is no water-tight division separating that sphere from the field covered by the Convention.[1]

This adds another element to general discussions about social and economic rights. What rights of such a character can be read into the texts already existing? The future will doubtless reveal, thanks to the skill and ingenuity of lawyers, further areas where, in present-day circumstances, there may be far more to be deduced from the original texts than had been thought say twenty years ago.

I turn now to a different topic, the international character of the European Convention. The most novel feature of the Convention thirty years ago was the prospect it opened up of a private individual being enabled to arraign a State, even his own, before an international tribunal. When the first case, an Irish one called *Lawless*, reached the Court in 1960, there was a story current in French diplomatic circles that about the time the final text of the Convention was being approved in Dublin, a civil servant had made a reassuring minute to a hesitant Minister before a cabinet meeting to the effect that no Irishman worthy of the name would even think of launching proceedings against his own country before the proposed international Commission! Unlike most anecdotes of this kind, that particular one has apparently been vouched for in private. However that may be, the story well reflects the attitudes prevailing in 1950.

In the early days of the operation of the Convention there is no doubt that Governments greeted with dismay the initial communication by the Commission of a complaint directed against them, they were consternated by a decision declaring a complaint admissible, and they regarded as an unmitigated and shameful disaster the reference, with the attendant publicity, of a case to the European Court. It says much for the tact and the painstaking and patently fairminded approach of the Commission and the Court over the years, that successive Governments in not a few countries gradually discarded their attitude of suspicion or distrust. The result is that to date not a single one has declined to renew the declarations accepting the jurisdiction of the Court and the right of individual petition to the Commission when the current ones expired. As more and more States have accepted the various competences of international tribunals over the years, the full operation of the European Convention has developed gradually and this impetus has been maintained.

It may be well, however, not to lose sight of nor take for granted this aspect of the Convention's international character.

since the question has a tendency to rebound in some countries. There has been some controversy in the columns of *The Times* recently (17 March 1980, for example) about renewing the United Kingdom's declarations early in 1981. In reply to a Parliamentary Question in January 1980[2] the Lord Privy Seal stated that 'at the appropriate time the decision of Her Majesty's Government will be communicated to Parliament'. The possibilities of initiating certain procedures are then subject to a decision by the Government concerned whether it will make the appropriate declarations. But the proceedings themselves, testing the observance of the engagements undertaken by the Contracting Parties, are clearly of an international character, addressed as they are to international bodies.

The European Convention, as a multilateral international treaty, provides a collective guarantee for the observance of the fundamental rights and freedoms contained therein. It thereby creates obligations binding on the states to make their domestic law and practices conform with the engagements undertaken, but without prescribing – in the form of directives or otherwise – how such conformity is to be achieved. In this sense, the Convention has no supranational character, and in fact various States have used different methods according to their own domestic systems. Similarly, the Convention does not provide any link between international proceedings and any national procedures that may precede them. Thus there is no way whereby a national court faced with an issue arising on the construction of the Convention, be it incorporated into domestic law or not, can refer that issue for a preliminary ruling to the Convention's organs. There is no provision corresponding to Article 177 of the EEC Treaty.

The rule laid down in Article 26 on the prior exhaustion of domestic remedies, is yet another illustration of the essentially international character of proceedings taken under the Convention. This rule has been strictly applied by the Convention's organs where the existence of a domestic remedy is clear. There can be no doubt that the relative inexistence of a chain of remedies, such as administrative courts in the United Kingdom, has resulted in cases against it reaching the admissibility stage before the European Commission much more speedily than would happen in respect of other States. In the *Golder* case[3], to cite just one example, a simple refusal by the Home Office to allow a person serving a long sentence for a serious crime to consult or write to a solicitor after he had been alleged to have taken part in a prison riot led directly to international proceedings. This is a zone where a Bill of Rights becomes relevant to the working of the European Convention, though it is, of course, no more than a secondary consideration.

The Convention leaves open the questions as to how the Contracting States should ensure the effective application of its provisions in their domestic law. Different ways and means may be chosen or adopted, and there is certainly no obligation to set up a constitutional control system. Such considerations point to and underline the subsidiary or supplementary nature of the International Treaty in relation to domestic law. The European Court of Human Rights has declared that it

> cannot assume the role of the competent national authorities, for it would thereby lose sight of the subsidiary nature of the international machinery of collective enforcement established by the Convention. The national authorities remain free to choose the measures which they consider appropriate in those matters which are governed by the Convention. Review by the Court concerns only the conformity of these measures with the requirements of the Convention.[4]

And again,

> The Court points out that the machinery of protection established by the Convention is subsidiary to the national systems safeguarding human rights. The Convention leaves to each Contracting State, in the first place, the task of securing the rights and freedoms it enshrines. The institutions created by it make their own contribution to this task but they become involved only through contentious proceedings and once all domestic remedies have been exhausted.[5]

Where the Convention itself provides for limitations or restrictions qualifying the enjoyment of a right there is a certain 'margin of appreciation' left to the Contracting States. Whilst conceding that national authorities, be they courts or other bodies, must in the first place assess whether a measure interfering with the enjoyment of the rights and freedoms guaranteed by the Convention is required in the public interest, both the European Court and the Commission see it as their duty to supervise such matters in order to ascertain that the restrictive measure has been exercised within the limits foreseen by the Convention. The doctrine first appeared in emergency type cases concerning the island of Cyprus before it attained independence and the *Lawless*[6] case. It has since been developed in the fields of education (Belgium), military discipline (Netherlands), and the *Sunday Times* Thalidomide case. It results in a rather strict degree of supervision although the boundaries of the concept will probably never be certain.

Here I will advert, if I may, to Clause 4 of the Bill of Rights brought from the House of Lords on 6 December 1979. The Clause stipulates that for the purposes of the Act, a declaration by Order in Council that there exists for the purposes of any derogating measures a time of war or other emergency threatening the life of the nation, shall be conclusive. This would mean that no court in the United Kingdom could look behind the declaration. However, the same would not be true of the European Commission and Court in the event of a case coming before them. And in the *Greek* case in 1969[7] the Commission found that the respondent Government had not satisfied it that there had been, in April 1967, a public emergency threatening the life of the Greek nation. It was not therefore necessary to go further and ascertain whether the measures of derogation taken etc. could be justified.

In conclusion, I would stress the *conciliatory* function of the Commission in proceedings under the European Convention. This function distinguishes them from ordinary contentious proceedings. Successful mediation by the Commission can even on occasion lead to resolving difficulties wider than the immediate issues raised in a particular case. There can be changes in law or in practice or a whole scheme of measures can be adopted. Furthermore, even in a country where the Convention is not part of the national legal order, its mere existence may temper official attitudes without it being possible in particular instances to point directly to cause and effect.

The European Convention in Operation

Member States and the European Convention on Human*

List of Member States of the Council of Europe	Ratification of Convention	Declarations under Article 25 recognising the Competence of the Commission to receive individual Petitions	Declarations under Article 46 recognising as compulsory the jurisdiction of the Court
Austria	✓	✓	✓
Belgium	✓	✓	✓
Cyprus	✓	–	✓
Denmark	✓	✓	✓
France	✓	–	✓
Fed. Rep. of Germany	✓	✓	✓
Greece	✓	–	✓
Iceland	✓	✓	✓
Ireland	✓	✓	✓
Italy	✓	✓	✓
Liechtenstein	–	–	–
Luxembourg	✓	✓	✓
Malta	✓	–	–
Netherlands	✓	✓	✓
Norway	✓	✓	✓
Portugal	✓	✓	✓
Spain	✓	–	✓
Sweden	✓	✓	✓
Switzerland	✓	✓	✓
Turkey	✓	–	–
United Kingdom	✓	✓	✓

*As at April 1980

ACCESSION OF THE EUROPEAN COMMUNITY TO THE EUROPEAN CONVENTION ON HUMAN RIGHTS

Dr C.-D. Ehlermann

The topic of Community accession to the European Convention on Human Rights raises compex issues. Before discussing the important political questions involved, it is useful to recall some of the essential characteristics of the European Community. Thereafter I shall look at the evolution of the protection of human rights at Community level, and at the various options available to the Community to enhance that protection. This will lead to an explanation of the principal reasons behind the Commission's choice of Community accession to the Convention. Understandably there are certain difficulties involved with this accession and they deserve consideration. Finally, I shall discuss some of the procedural aspects relating to Community accession to the Convention on Human Rights.

1 Characteristics of the European Community

It is worth recalling at the outset some of the essential and unique characteristics of the European Community.[1] First, the European Community has its own legal personality. It is a distinct entity from the nine Member States which created it. The Treaties establishing the Community are in fact its constitution. It is important to remember that the Community, unlike sovereign States, does not have limitless powers. Rather, it has power to act only in those areas where competence has been transferred to it by the Member States. The primary fields of activity and objectives of the Community are, it is true, essentially economic – but the Community is also a political venture.

The institutions of the Community may only act within the framework and in the areas laid down in the Treaties; their powers are, therefore, limited. But it is worth stressing that the Community is not a static entity – it is evolving, and consequentially creating new rights and obligations for its citizens in new fields of activity. Thus the Community can adopt legislation which *directly* creates rights and obligations for citizens within the Member States without any intervention by national Parliaments. Equally it can adopt Community rules which the Member States are *bound* to implement through national measures. All the rights thus created are protected by the different national courts and by the Court of Justice in Luxembourg.

It is against this background that the question of human rights at Community level must be studied. What is at stake is the compatibility of Community rules with fundamental rights – an important political problem.

2 The Evolution of Community Protection of Human Rights

The Community is not a member of the European Convention on Human Rights. This is hardly astonishing as the Convention is only open to States – the Member States of the Council of Europe.

It is interesting to note that there is no overt or general treatment of 'the protection of fundamental rights' in the Treaties establishing the Community. However, certain individual examples of such rights may be found in the Treaties, for example the prohibition on discrimination on grounds of nationality (Article 7 of the EEC Treaty) and the requirement that men and women should receive equal pay for equal work (Article 119 of the EEC Treaty). The traditional explanation for this runs along the lines that the powers of the Community were largely limited to economic fields, so that it was most unlikely that Community rules could infringe on basic human rights. It would, however, be wrong to conclude that the question of human rights was completely absent from the spirit of the founding fathers of the Community. Indeed they solemnly declared in the Preamble to the EEC Treaty that they were resolved, by the pooling of their resources, to preserve and strengthen peace and liberty. Liberty, in our understanding, manifestly includes respect for Human Rights.

The question of an alleged violation of human rights by the Community was raised as long ago as the late fifties. The Court of Justice in Luxembourg was the first Community institution which had to tackle the question. The Court had to deal with a

complaint that a particular Community act violated a fundamental right guaranteed by the constitution of a Member State –
to be precise the Constitution of the Federal Rupublic of
Germany. The first reaction of the Court was a cautious one
indeed. The Court felt that it was not its role to test the validity of
Community rules against the rules laid down in the Constitutions
of the Member States.[2] At that very early stage, the Court did not
say anything about the protection of fundamental rights by
Community law itself.

Happily this rather restrictive attitude of the Court changed in
the late sixties. The court ruled[3] that respect for fundamental
rights formed an *integral* part of the general principles of law, the
observance of which it had to ensure. In 1974 the Court declared[4]
that it could not accept measures that were incompatible with the
fundamental rights recognised and protected by the constitutions
of the Member States. It also stated that, similarly, international
treaties for the protection of human rights (such as the European
Convention on Human Rights) can supply *guidelines* which
should be followed within the framework of Community Law.
However, the Court has not yet formally declared that the
Community is bound by the provisions of the Convention.[5]

It is interesting to have regard to the kinds of circumstances in
which possible violations of human rights have been·alleged or
suggested before the Court of Justice. In one case[6], a decision of
the Commission concerning measures to make butter available
to certain categories of consumers (who were beneficiaries under
a social welfare scheme, and whose income did not allow them to
buy it at the normal prices) was attacked as constituting a
violation of human rights, on the ground that it contained a
provision under which the names of the beneficiaries had to be
divulged to retailers. In another case[7] there was a challenge
against a decision made by the authorities in France which
denied the right of residence to an Italian migrant worker in
certain areas (*Departments*) of France since his trade union
activities in those areas appeared to be prejudicial to public
policy. This was challenged as contravening a basic human right
to move freely within a State and to choose one's place of
residence.

Another example is to be found in a case[8] where a candidate
for employment with the Council of Ministers was unable, for

religious reasons, to sit a prescribed examination on a particular day. The refusal of the Council to fix another date was challenged on the ground that it amounted to religious discrimination. A final example is provided by a very recent case[9] where a Council regulation which curtailed the right to plant new vines during a certain period of time, was challenged as being a violation of the right of ownership.

It is also important to note the reaction of some of the national courts to the possibility of Community acts violating fundamental rights which were guaranteed by their national constitutions. In May 1974, the German Constitutional Court[10] declared that so long as there existed no Community catalogue of fundamental rights corresponding to the German Constitution, it was entitled to decide upon the applicability of legal acts of the Community – even where those had previously been declared lawful by the Court of Justice in Luxembourg. The Italian Constitutional Court in 1973[11], while not going quite so far, had expressed a similar concern. Though such an approach is certainly not compatible with the principle of the unity of Community law, nor with the exclusive right of the Court of Justice in Luxembourg to review Community legislation, it demonstrated clearly that certain of the supreme courts in the Member States were much preoccupied by the absence of any written catalogue of human rights which was guaranteed at Community level.

Amongst the Community's political institutions, it was the European Parliament which was most concerned with human rights during the seventies. The Parliament was aware of and understood the case law of the Court of Justice; but it believed that there was a need for even more effective protection of fundamental rights at Community level. Amongst the Members of the Parliament there was strong support for the idea of a *special* Community Charter of human rights; they also approved[12] the idea of Community accession to the Convention.

The first reaction of the Commission to the suggestion that there should be accession (a suggestion emanating from various quarters), was a rather cautious one. Initially, the Commission pointed to the case-law of the Court of Justice. It stated[13] that the Court of Justice was doing excellent work in the field of human rights and argued that the developing case-law provided the best way of defining and protecting human rights in Community law.

It also said that it believed that the Community was bound by the substantive provisions of the Convention. Some years later, however, the Commission took the initiative in proposing a Joint Declaration of the European Parliament, the Council of Ministers and itself. This Joint Declaration[14] stressed the prime importance of the protection of fundamental rights and the intention of the three political Community institutions to respect those rights.

Another impetus for further action came during the discussions about the *enlargement* of the Community. All the Community institutions share the conviction that Spain, Portugal and Greece, which have so recently (re)established democratic regimes, wish strongly and by all possible means, to avoid a return to dictatorship. The European Parliament made known its position on the link between the maintenance of democracy and membership of the Community. The Parliament demanded[15] that

the present Member States of the European Community, together with the applicant States, give a formal undertaking to uphold the provisions governing civil and political rights and pluralist democracy embodied in their respective national laws and in the international treaties to which they are signatories and asks that the failure to respect these provisions, to be established by the Court of Justice, should constitute incompatibility with Membership of the Community.

It is against this background that one must consider the Declaration[16] of the European Council, adopted in 1978, in which the Heads of State or Government of the nine Member States solemnly declare ʻthat respect for and maintenance of representative democracy and human rights in each Member State are essential elements of membership of the European Communities'.

In addition, there was, over the years, increasing pressure from public opinion, in particular as manifested in the European Parliament, in favour of a written catalogue of human rights which would be *binding* on the Community. Public opinion has not been fully satisfied – either by the various declarations made on human rights, or by the praiseworthy work done by the Court of Justice in that field. A strong body of opinion argues for even greater security and protection. Faced with this situation, the *political institutions* cannot remain unresponsive or passive. It is not sufficient for them to sit back and rely on the eventuality of the Court of Justice having the opportunity to rapidly develop relevant case law to cover a wide spectrum of human rights matters.

The Commission of the European Community has in fact not been inactive. Indeed it has taken a major new political initiative in the field of human rights at Community level. It has responded to the growing demand for the citizens of Europe to know unambiguously which fundamental rights *are* guaranteed at Community level and which *cannot* be infringed by the Community Institutions. It has recommended in a recent Memorandum[17] that the Community as such should become a Contracting Party to the Convention.

3 The Options Available

The various options available to the Community, and which the Commission could have recommended for adoption, may be briefly summarised.

(a) First, the Commission could have recommended that the Community adopt a *special* Charter of human rights *legally* binding on the Community Institutions. The Commission is aware of the advantages of a new catalogue which could be freshly drafted and specially adapted to the needs of the Community. Indeed it is in favour of such a catalogue in the long term. However it considers that it is not realistic to expect that, within a reasonable period of time, Member States could agree on such a delicate and complicated subject as a new charter of human rights. If the operation were undertaken with too much haste there is a danger that significant differences might emerge between the Member States – perhaps particularly as regards economic and social rights. Such a situation could lead to a situation where only the lowest common denominator could be agreed upon. This would be a retrograde step compared with the level of protection already guaranteed by the Court of Justice in Luxembourg. It is important to note, in this respect, that the first attempts to incorporate economic and social rights into the European Convention on Human Rights were not at all successful. Taking account of such factors, the Commission decided that this is not the appropriate moment for embarking on such an enterprise. (Although, of course, accession to the European Convention does not prevent such a catalogue being introduced in the future.) Furthermore, the Commission has accepted that the initiative in constructing a special Community Charter should, in the first place, come from the European Parliament.

(b) Second, the Commission could have simply turned towards the European Parliament suggesting that as the body representing the citizens of Europe, it should draw up a resolution containing a Charter of human rights to be respected by the Community Institutions. It is true that since its members have been directly elected, the Parliament has gained a new legitimacy. The change in election methods did not, however, serve to add or introduce any legislative powers which (with certain exceptions as regards the Commission) continue to lie with the Council of Ministers. Nevertheless the Parliament could draw up a comprehensive catalogue of rights that could be contained in a Parliamentary resolution. The Commission and the Council of Ministers could then give a political undertaking to respect the rights laid down in the Charter adopted by the Parliament. Yet there is a major weakness in such a possible solution – it is that the Parliament has no power to adopt a legally binding Charter. That is, the Parliament's Charter would only have a *political* impact which, while no doubt very important, is not sufficient to improve effectively the protection of human rights at Community level.

From such considerations flows the conclusion that *both* a special legally binding catalogue for the Community, and any catalogue adopted by the European Parliament (without legal effect) should be *preceded* by Community accession to the European Convention on Human Rights. Uniformity in the protection of human rights within Western Europe may be served best in this way.

(c) Third, it would of course be legally possible for the Community to adopt, by an autonomous act, the substantive provisions[18] of the Convention. Within the legal order of the Community, the relevant institutions would be formally bound to respect the Convention and not to violate it by their actions. The compatibility of the acts of the institutions *vis-à-vis* the substantive provisions of the Convention would be controlled by the Court of Justice in Luxembourg. This solution would ensure that individuals could rely on the terms of the Convention when challenging Community acts before either the national Courts or the Court of Justice in Luxembourg. The principal objection to this solution lies in the fact that there would be no *international judicial control* of the actions of the Community Institutions with regard to their compatibility with the provisions of the Convention. The Commission has taken the view that such control is a vital element in the protection of human rights.

(d) Fourth, the Commission could have suggested that (possibly in addition to the provisions of the Convention becoming part of Community law through an autonomous act of the latter) a special link be set up between the Court of Justice in Luxembourg and the European Court of Human Rights in Strasbourg. It would, theoretically, be possible to work out a system whereby, if the Court of Justice in Luxembourg found itself confronted with a problem which required an interpretation of the provisions of the Convention, it would ask for an opinion of the Court in Strasbourg. Yet there do not seem to be sufficiently strong arguments in favour of such a special link. Within the context of the Community's relationship with the Council of Europe and with the Convention on Human Rights (concluded within the latter's framework) the Court of Justice should, properly speaking, be considered as an *internal jurisdiction*. It therefore seems logical that, as regards the Convention, the Court of Justice in Luxembourg should not be treated differently from the highest domestic Courts of the other Contracting Parties to the Convention.

(e) After weighing the competing considerations and evaluating the options, the Commission decided in favour of a more simple but also more radical solution. As already mentioned, it has recommended in its recent Memorandum that the Community as such should become a Contracting Party to the Convention. This would mean that the Convention would be legally binding on the institutions of the Community, and that their *acts* would ultimately be subject to the control of the bodies set up under the Convention.

The Commission's recommendation, it should be made clear, does not coincide with an idea once put forward within the European Parliament. Here it was suggested that, once the Community Treaties had been amended to include the Convention, then not only would the Community Institutions be bound by the Convention, but the Community would *also* acquire the right to control the actions of the Member States as regards their compatibility with the fundamental rights enshrined in the Convention in *all* fields, even in areas outside the competence of the Community. It is necessary to dispel any notion that this is what the Commission has recommended. Such a suggestion would certainly not be considered feasible by the Member States. For them it would be an unacceptable extension of the role of the Community into areas outside its powers. It is, therefore, most important to understand that what the Commission recommends in its Memorandum on Community Accession to the Convention is limited to the *legal acts of the Community institutions themselves.*

4 The Commission's Reasoning

Of all the factors which led the Commission to opt for full participation by the Community in the European Convention on Human Rights, only the principal reasons need to be rehearsed here.

(a) First, the Commission was convinced that the European Convention on Human Rights represents one of the outstanding achievements of the Council of Europe. Nothing should be done to weaken or detract from that achievement. If the Community went ahead and sought to draw up its own Charter on human rights *before* acceding to the Convention, it could be seen as an indirect rejection of the Convention, or as implying that it was out of date. The European Convention and the measures taken by the Court of Justice in Luxembourg to protect basic rights both, essentially, espouse the same aim – that it is the protection of a heritage of fundamental and human rights considered inalienable by democratic European States. The protection of this Western European heritage should ultimately be uniform and accordingly assigned to the bodies specifically set up for this purpose; this applies to the Community as much as to sovereign States. The Community is now sufficiently mature and developed to be able to submit its activities to an international jurisdiction in the field of human rights.

(b) Accession to the Convention would make a substantial contribution to the strengthening of democratic beliefs and freedoms both within and beyond the free world. Even more than the joint Declaration by the three political institutions made on

5 April 1977 on the protection of fundamental rights [19], it would make clear to the whole world that the Community does not merely make political declarations of intent. Rather it would evidence its determination to provide real guarantees of the protection of human rights by binding itself to a written catalogue of fundamental freedoms.

(c) Third, the fact that the Community itself was a Contracting Party to the Convention would, I suggest, help to maintain democratic regimes within the Member States during times of difficulty. It is illogical that respect for human rights is a condition of membership of the Community, but the Community itself is not a Member of the Convention. If the Community acceded to the Convention and if problems subsequently arose within a Member State, it is quite possible that the other Member States would prefer to tackle the delicate problems involved within a Community framework rather than bilaterally.

(d) Fourth, and this is perhaps a more practical reason, all the Member States of the Community are also Contracting Parties to the Convention. They have, therefore, all agreed to the substantive provisions of the Convention. This has the large advantage for the Community of avoiding any need to start negotiations on the contents of a new (and different) catalogue of human rights.

(e) Fifth, the Commission believes that the rights guaranteed by the European Convention *are relevant* to the activities of the Community. At first sight it might, perhaps, appear that a Convention, which essentially deals with traditional freedoms, would not be of particular relevance to a Community devoted, in the main, to economic objectives. Upon closer examination, however, it can be seen that the Convention is indeed relevant. Further, as already mentioned, accession to the Convention will not in any way preclude the Community working towards its own Charter – one specially adapted to its needs. Equally accession will not prevent the Court of Justice in Luxembourg from continuing to develop its already excellent case-law in the field of human rights, particularly in defining economic and social rights which are barely touched upon in the Convention. It is quite clear that the European Convention on Human Rights is only a *minimum* code, which thus does not, in any way, prevent its Contracting Parties from developing more extensive protections of human rights.

Returning now to the relevance of the European Convention to the activities of the Community, some examples have already been given of cases coming before the Court of Justice in Luxembourg where violation of human rights was claimed to have taken place. It is not difficult to identify other hypothetical circumstances where Community rules could come into conflict with the rights guaranteed by the Convention. It might be worth illustrating how the Convention could be relevant to Community activities – but they are purely theoretical examples and in no way represent concrete plans of the Commission!

(i) *Article 6* which guarantees 'due process' – the right to a fair and public hearing by an independent and impartial tribunal – could be relevant not only to proceedings before the Court of Justice in Luxembourg, but also to certain procedures in the Commission, for example, in the field of competition.

(ii) *Article 7* is the expression of the principle *'nulla poene sine lege'*. It has quite recently been invoked in a case[20] in which the Commission imposed a fine for violation of Article 85 of the EEC Treaty.

(iii) *Article 8* guarantees the respect for private and family life, the home, and correspondence. It could play a role, for example, in situations similar to the Stauder case already mentioned.[21] Equally it might be relevant if, in the area of free movement of people, the Community were to adopt restrictive rules *vis-à-vis* the family. Or again it could be invoked in the area of competition and transport, where Community law offers considerable possibilities of investigation.

(iv) *Article 9* protects freedom of thought, conscience and religion.[22] This could, for example, prove relevant if the Community one day tried to harmonise the non-working days within the Member States. The Community has in fact already taken religious rites into consideration – for instance in a 1964 Council directive on inter-Community trade in fresh meat and its provisions on slaughtering.[23]

(v) *Article 10* concerns freedom of expression and could be relevant in cases of harmonisation of restrictive measures concerning media productions (films, literature and the like) of a political nature.

(vi) *Article 11* guarantees freedom of association, especially as regards trade unions. It would be relevant if the Community were to take measures to set the limits between the right to strike on the one hand, and the obligations flowing from the free movement of goods on the other. There has in fact already been a written question (No. 909/79) to the Commission on this topic from a member of the European Parliament.[24]

(vii) *Article 13* gives a right to an effective remedy. It is clear that this provision has implications for the Community. Indeed it poses a problem given the limits imposed by the Treaties on direct actions by individuals before the Court of Justice.

(viii) *Article 1* of Protocol 1 to the Convention guarantees private property. Its importance for the Community is patently clear – as may be seen from the recent judgment of the Court in Luxembourg in the Hauer case concerning the prohibition on planting vines.[25]

(ix) The provisions of the Fourth Protocol to the Convention which relate to the free movement of people are obviously relevant to the Community in ways which require no explanation.

(f) A sixth reason which weighed with the Commission was as follows. On the basis of the present legal relationship between the Community and the Convention (in particular the fact that the Community is not a Contracting Party to the Convention) it seems impossible for the Community to be made the direct object of an application either by a State or individual. Yet it is *a priori* conceivable that the acts of the Community might be called into question before the European Commission of Human Rights or the Court of Human Rights indirectly via the Member States of the Community. It is necessary here to distinguish two eventualities. First, the possibility of Community acts being indirectly challenged in Strasbourg is especially evident where Community rules are implemented by national measures without any discretion being left to the Member States. These national measures could certainly be challenged in Strasbourg, but then what is really at stake is the compatibility of the Community rules (which underpin the national measures) with the European Convention. Second, a Community act, where there is no implementing national measure, might be challenged. Such a situation arose in 1978 when an application[26] was brought by an employee's association which sought to incriminate *all* the

Member States together, concerning a decision of the Council of Ministers. Admittedly this application was dismissed by the European Commission of Human Rights, but only on grounds which related to the particular circumstances of the case. One cannot therefore rule out the possibility of the European Commission or the European Court of Human Rights one day taking a different view of the collective responsibility of the Member States of the Community.

If Community rules can be impugned either through individual Member States or through Member States collectively, surely it is more correct for the Community to become a full Contracting Party to the Convention so that it can then defend directly any of its actions which are called into question before the Commission or Court in Strasbourg.

(g) Seventh, Community accession to the Convention would result in a real improvement to the protection of the rights of individual citizens at Community level. It would provide them with a written catalogue of fundamental rights which they would know could not be violated by the Community institutions. At present citizens of the member countries of the Community can only rely on the decision-making of the Court of Justice in Luxembourg – but of course the outcome of cases before the Court cannot be predicted with certainty. If the Community became a Contracting Party to the Convention, both the national courts and the Court of Justice in Luxembourg would be obliged to satisfy themselves in cases before them which involved Community actions that those acts were compatible with the rights guaranteed under the Convention. In addition, the in-dividual would have the further protection of the controls exercised by the Strasbourg bodies set up under the Convention. (The question of the Community accepting individual applica-tions against its actions is discussed below.)

(h) Finally, the extra protection afforded to citizens through the written catalogue of rights contained in the European Convention, would reduce the risk (referred to above) of national courts using the absence of a written catalogue of fundamental rights, formally binding upon the Community, as a justificaton for reviewing acts of the Council of Ministers or the Commission according to the provisions of their national constitutions.

3 Difficulties Concerning Community Accession to the European Convention

In recommending that the Community should adhere to the European Convention, the Commission did not underestimate the difficult questions such a course of action poses. The major difficulties can be discussed under three categories.

A Difficulties resulting from the legal order of the Community

(a) The Commission has continuously stressed, in reply to questions raised, that the mere fact that the Community accedes to the Convention will not result in an extension of the powers of the Community. It will not in any way mean that the Community would become a sort of international policeman in the field of human rights (particularly *vis-à-vis* its own Member States) in all fields of activity including those outside the present scope of the Community's powers. On the contrary, accession to the Convention would instead imply a limitation on the activities of the Community Institutions. Their activities would be subordinated to the provisions of the Convention. The aim of accession, therefore, lies in ensuring proper controls over Community actions. The implementation of national measures by the Member States in fulfilment of their Community obligations would not be affected by Community accession to the Convention.

(b) Accession to the Convention would not result in any upheaval of the institutional structures of the Community. In acceding to the Convention the Community would be like a sovereign State, acting as a subject of international law. It would be submitting its activities to a specialised control machinery in the field of human rights; it would be joining together with a large group of countries to ensure unity and uniformity in the field of human rights in Western Europe. And there is nothing anomalous in the idea that the Community should submit its activities to international control. Indeed it has already been prepared to do so under the terms of several Conventions signed with third countries, for example, in the first Lomé Convention signed in 1975 between African, Caribbean, and Pacific countries and the Community.

(c) As regards the legal basis for the Community's power to

accede to the Convention, the Commission has a rather open-minded approach. It believes that it is currently possible for the Community to accede to the Convention on the basis of the existing Treaties setting up the Community. On the other hand, it would see no fundamental objection to the Treaties being modified to formally provide for accession to the Convention.

B Difficulties resulting from the division of powers between the Community and its Member States

The question of the effects which Community accession to the European Convention would have on the status of the Convention within the municipal legal orders of the Members has already emerged as an important issue. This question is of particular importance for countries like the United Kingdom where the Convention is not part of domestic law and thus may not be invoked in their domestic courts, except as an aid to statutory interpretation. It is, therefore, necessary to clarify certain points on this issue.

(a) As already stated, the aim behind Community accession to the Convention is to ensure the compatibility of Community acts with the rights guaranteed under the Convention. The aim is not, therefore, to control national measures taken by the Member States in implementation of their Community obligations. In certain cases the Member States are left no discretionary power over the implementation of their Community obligations; but even in these circumstances the implementing measures of the Member States would not be ' affected' by Community accession to the Convention.

(b) It follows from this that Community accession to the Convention will not change the status of the Convention within the domestic legal orders of the Member States. In the United Kingdom, for example, should the Community become a Contracting Party to the Convention, then the provisions of the latter would become part of Community law; individuals could thus, under the Community's legal system, invoke the provisions of the European Convention before the Courts of the United Kingdom to challenge actions of the Community institutions. But they could only challenge those acts and not measures introduced by the United Kingdom authorities in implementation of their Community obligations.

(c) Just as Community accession to the European Convention will not affect the status of the Convention within the domestic legal orders of Member States, similarly accession will not affect the Reservations (i.e. limitations to the obligations accepted) to certain Articles in the Convention which were made by different Member States when they became Contracting Parties to it. These Reservations will continue to be applicable as regards all national measures, including those taken in furtherance of Community obligations. As far as the Community is concerned all Reservations made by it would be applicable to Community acts. In the Commission's opinion, if the Community does accede to the Convention, then it should not 'accumulate' the Reservations made by the Member States, but should, rather, only enter the Reservations which are necessary because of the Community's own legal structure.

(d) Another important issue on which difficulties could arise, because of the varying attitudes of the Member States, is whether the Community should allow individuals to make applications against its acts to the Commission of Human Rights in Strasbourg, thereby setting in motion the entire gamut of procedures followed by the Commission of Human Rights and the Court of Human Rights. This right of individuals to make applications is not automatic under the Convention; each of the Contracting Parties has to decide whether or not it is prepared to allow such applications against their national laws. If a Contracting Party does not accept this possibility, then its actions can only be challenged in Strasbourg by another State which is a Contracting Party to the Convention.

At present, all the Member States of the Community, with the exception of France, have accepted the individual right of petition against their domestic actions. The Commission is in favour of the Community also accepting such right of petition against its own acts. If the Community did decide to do so, however, this would not affect the positions taken by the Member States on this point as regards their national measures. Legally speaking, therefore, it is conceivable that in France, for example, an individual would have the right to challenge Community acts before the Commission of Human Rights, but he could not challenge measures adopted by the French authorities.

Politically, however, this 'double status' for individual petitions within certain Member States (Greece, which will become a Member of the Community in 1981, has also not accepted individual petitions) might not be acceptable to the Member States concerned. For this reason, the Commission considers that if there are difficulties for the nine Member States in accepting the right of individual petitions against Community acts, such a right is not a *sine qua non* for the Community to open negotiations concerning its accession to the Convention. It is even conceivable that the Community could become a Contracting Party to the Convention without such a right being accepted from the very moment of ratification. However, the Commission firmly believes that if Community accession to the Convention is to have its full political and legal impact as regards the protection of fundamental rights at Community level, then the Community must accept, as soon as possible after accession, the individual right of petition.

C Difficulties concerning Community participation in the European Convention proceedings

(a) The European Commission of Human Rights is composed of a number of Members equal to the number of Contracting Parties to the Convention. The European Court of Human Rights is composed of a number of Members equal to that of the number of Contracting Parties to the Council of Europe. The Members of both these bodies act in their individual capacity and are therefore not bound by the instructions of any government. The question therefore arises whether it would be necessary that a 'Community' Commissioner and a 'Community' judge be added to these bodies or whether it would be possible after Community accession to leave them with their present composition.

The Commission has opted for a solution whereby another Member would be added to both bodies following Community accession to the Convention. The principal reasons why the Commission has adopted this position are that such a solution corresponds best to the need to underline the independent legal capacity of the Community, and that the members of the Commission of Human Rights and the Court of Human Rights are not necessarily sufficiently familiar with the Community legal system. (There are certain detailed technical problems which arise as regards the mode of election of the Community 'representative' to the two bodies. These are dealt with in the Commission's Memorandum.[27])

(b) For the Committee of Ministers of the Council of Europe, the Commission has proposed a more radical solution. It suggests that it would be appropriate to exclude the Committee of Ministers totally from proceedings relating to Community matters. Although its functions are quasi-judicial, the Committee of Ministers is a political body whose Members are bound by instructions from their respective governments. It is hardly conceivable that the Community and the Member States could hold divergent views within the Committee, and the other Contracting Parties might thus find all decisions that called Community acts into question, blocked. On the other hand a position whereby the Member States would have to withdraw from decision-making where a Community act was in question could not be accepted – this would reduce their role abnormally. Further, as the Commission recommends the Community should accept the compulsory jurisdiction of the European Court of Human Rights, the question of the representation of the Community within the Committee loses all practical importance.

6 Procedures Relating to Community Accession to the Convention

After a general and no doubt wide-ranging discussion has taken place within the Community, the Commission will decide whether to make a formal recommendation to the Council of Ministers that it should proceed to open negotiations on the accession of the Community to the European Convention. Up until now there have been no discussions within the Council of Ministers on the Commission's Memorandum on Community accession to the Convention. It would appear that the Council of Ministers prefers to await the opinion of the European Parliament before starting its own consideration. This is a wise decision on the part of the Council.

As already mentioned, the 'old' European Parliament stated that it was, in principle, in favour of Community accession to the Convention. The 'new' directly elected Parliament will certainly form an opinion on the ideas contained in the Commission's Memorandum. The Economic and Social Committee of the

Community is also preparing its opinion. The Court of Justice has adopted a rather prudent attitude to the Commission's Memorandum– it recognises that accession to the Convention is a political issue.

If the Commission does formally recommend accession to the Convention, then, prior to negotiations being started with the Contracting Parties to the Convention, there would have to be a unanimous decision by the Council of Ministers of the Community in favour of such negotiations being opened. If negotiations were begun, they would concentrate on the amendments which would have to be made to the Convention to take account of the fact that the Community is not a sovereign State. As mentioned above, membership of the Convention is at present limited to participation of sovereign States who are Members of the Council of Europe. The Commission has expressed the view, in its Memorandum, that it is unlikely that fundamental amendments to the provisions of the Convention will prove necessary. Once the terms of Community participation have been agreed, a protocol permitting Community accession to the Convention would have to be ratified by all the Contracting Parties to the Convention. As far as the Community is concerned, it may prove necessary to amend the Treaties establishing the Community so that the Community, itself, can then ratify the Convention. This whole process will obviously take several years.

Conclusion

The Commission's recommendation that the European Community should accede to the European Convention on Human Rights is, I realise, an ambitious project. But the objective is eminently worthwhile – the enhancement of the protection of human rights throughout the Community. After all one must not see the Community in an arid vacuum. It is essential that the Community should be understood to care about the most essential aspects of the welfare of all Community citizens – the protection of their fundamental rights. If the political will emerges amongst the nine Member States and the other Contracting Parties in favour of Community accession to the Convention any technical difficulties can be overcome.

BILLS OF RIGHTS: SOME ALTERNATIVES

Professor J. E. S. Fawcett

The proposal that a Bill of Rights be adopted for the United Kingdom poses a number of basic and related questions:

1 Should its provisions have the force of law, or be only a set of directive principles?
2 If given the force of law, should its provisions rank as higher law or only as any other statutory provisions?
3 What form should it take?
4 To whom should it be addressed?

No one of these questions can be fully answered without assumptions as to the answers to the others. Some assumptions and answers will be suggested here.

1 Should its provisions have the force of law, or be only a set of directive principles?

The Bill of Rights might be constructed as a set of directive principles for legislation. Two models might be considered. The Constitution of India (1949) has, in addition to a number of specific rights and freedoms set out in entrenched provisions in Part III, directive principles in Part IV, which are expressly declared to be not enforceable in the Courts, but to be nevertheless 'fundamental in the governance of the country, and it shall be the duty of the State to apply these principles in making laws' (s. 37). These directive principles of State policy, as might be expected given the contents of Part III, fall largely in the fields of economic and social rights and claims.

A similar idea is expressed in proposals for the revision of the Swiss Constitution, at present under consideration. A proposed draft Constitution has two Articles setting out certain principles and basic rights, and then provision for the enactment of specific legislation to implement them. The two Articles set out four general principles, and a number of basic rights by titular description only. The four general principles are that:

— Human dignity is inviolable (die Menschenwürde ist
  untastbar),
— the basic rights shall govern all exercise of public authority;
— the exercise of basic rights shall not be to the harm of others,
  or prevented by others, and shall not imperil the existence
  of the State;
— the State shall, to the extent of its financial resources,
  promote the exercise of basic rights.

The particular basic rights, listed by title only in much the same
manner as in the Canadian Bill of Rights (1960) s. 1, comprise
the traditional civil and political liberties and also rights to
education, to work and professional pursuits, to housing and to
social security.

In both systems then, the stated principles and titles of rights
and freedoms would serve as guidelines for future legislation.

*2 If given the force of law, should its provisions rank as higher
law or only as any other statutory provisions?*

On the assumption, however, that the new Bill of Rights would
have the force of law – an assumption drawn from the current
debates – it must be asked whether it would be made *higher law*
in that its provisions would override both prior and subsequent
legislation, as well as common law rules, if there was found to be
a conflict between them and provisions of the Bill. But there are
obstacles to the adoption of a Bill of Rights as higher law, that are
presented by the legislative supremacy of Parliament. This
supremacy appears to rest on two principles: that no Parliament
is bound or limited by Acts of its predecessors or by its own
earlier Acts, and that the statutes enacted by Parliament and in
force at any time are the highest law in that they alter or nullify
any common law rules or earlier statutory provisions that are
inconsistent with them. But no statute embodies these principles;
and the first principle cannot be derived from the common law,
for it could then be abolished under the second principle. The
principles are in fact *political axioms,* which form the base of
government of the United Kingdom.

Suppose then that Parliament enacted a Bill of Rights,
constituted as higher law in the sense past described; what would
be the position if a subsequent statute, expressly or by implication,

repealed any of its provisions? Under the first principle the later statute would prevail. But there are ways round this obstacle. In the first place, there would be strong political constraints upon an attempt to change or nullify the provisions of a Bill of Rights once adopted, even if they were not entrenched as higher law. Such action would be difficult to defend in Parliament or the constituencies, save in a situation of emergency or political instability. Further, the statute enacting the Bill of Rights might provide, as a first line of legal defence, that any subsequent statute inconsistent with its provisions would require a special majority for its adoption.[1] In Canada the Bill of Rights, adopted in 1960, was made higher law subject to possible subsequent legislation. The Act provided that:

> Every law of Canada shall, unless it is expressly declared by an Act of the Parliament of Canada that it shall operate notwithstanding the Canadian Bill of Rights, be so construed and applied as not to abrogate, abridge or to authorise the abrogation, abridgement or infringement of, any of the rights or freedoms herein recognized and declared....

3 What form should it take?

On the assumption again that the new Bill of Rights would have the force of law, it might be formed in a number of ways by:

(i) incorporation of the European Convention on Human Rights, with some amendments, into domestic law;

(ii) incorporation of the United Nations Civil and Political Rights Covenant, with some amendments, into domestic law;

(iii) composition of a new text, using the best provisions of both Convention and Covenant, and other principles not included in them.

(i) *Incorporation of the European Convention* would have the advantages of simplicity and some familiarity. Thirteen of the twenty Convention countries have taken this course.[2] But as they also all have, to a great extent, specific constitutional provisions protecting rights and freedoms, the impact of incorporation has been less than it would be in the United Kingdom.

The Convention comprises, as its substantive provisions, Articles 1-12, 14, 16-18 of the Convention itself, and Articles 1-

3 of the First Protocol, and Articles 1-4 of the Fourth Protocol. The United Kingdom has not yet ratified the Fourth Protocol. The main provisions are already thirty years old and reflect a different social climate from what is likely to prevail in the last quarter of the century. Some amendments could be useful in an incorporated text, if only to remove ambiguities that have been revealed or to fill gaps. For example, in the present texts it can be asked:

— How far does the right to life under Article 2 extend to the unborn child?
— Does the determination of whether detention is 'lawful' under Article 5 extend to the grounds of detention, or is it limited to the procedure?
— What is to be understood by 'civil rights and obligations' in Article 6?
— How far does 'family life' extend in Article 8 (does it, for example, extend to unmarried fathers, grandparents)?
— Are the restrictions permitted under Articles 8-11 for the 'protection of morals' limited to *public* morals?
— Does 'freedom of association' in Article 11 exclude the 'closed shop'?
— Is Article 17 adequate for the control of the irregular fighter?
— What does 'possessions/biens' mean in Article 1 of the First Protocol, and can the Article as it stands give any effective protection to property?

Further, Articles 13 (remedies for Convention breaches) and 15 (emergency derogations) would need some elaboration within the United Kingdom system.

(ii) *Incorporation of the United Nations Civil and Political Rights Covenant* (Articles 2-27) would have the advantage that some of its principles at least are better elaborated than the equivalent in the European Convention. However, the critical provision for liberty and security of person (Article 5(1)) is wholly inadequate. The United Kingdom has ratified the Covenant, with some reservations, concerning largely territories outside the United Kingdom, for which it is responsible. Again some amendments of the Covenant would be necessary for effective incorporation.

(iii) *The Composition of a New Text,* though still based in large part on the provisions of the Convention and the Covenant, could nevertheless achieve a number of purposes. These include amendment or adjustment of their provisions, possible provisions for special categories of person, and possible adaptations for the different regions of the British Isles.

Some amendments of the Convention or Covenant have already been suggested. Their extension might also be considered: for example, the new Bill of Rights might include some of the provisions of the European Social Charter. Special provisions for certain categories of person might be included covering, for example, the rights and duties of journalists, or the medical profession, or particular groups or associations. Finally, some adaptations or extensions of the Bill might be considered for one or more of the component regions: England, Scotland, Wales, Northern Ireland, Isle of Man and Channel Islands. Rockall needs no human rights.

4 To whom should the new Bill of Rights be addressed?

This question is asking in effect who is to be responsible for the observance and application of the new Bill of Rights. Here we may consider the position of Parliament, central government, local government, the courts and the Parliamentary Commissioners. A number of possibilities suggest themselves.

The Bill might be directed solely to the control of legislation, that is to say, by Parliament itself or by the courts. In a number of countries there can be a preliminary examination of Parliamentary Bills to see whether they may not conform with the Constitution and particularly its basic rights provisions. In the Federal Republic of Germany an Act may, before it actually enters into force, be referred by not less than one-third of the members of the Bundestag to the Federal Constitutional Court for a determination of the compatibility of any of its provisions with the *Grundgesetz* (Basic Law) (1949). In France Parliamentary Bills may be referred before their adoption for a similar purpose to a *Conseil Constitutionnel.* In both cases a finding that any of the clauses of the Act or Bill is contrary to the constitution, including the basic rights provisions, invalidates that clause. Belgium has the same practice but the finding takes the form of an advisory opinion to Parliament, which is not necessarily bound by it. In Singapore, under its Constitution Amendment Act

(1969), a constitutional council is enabled to draw the attention of the legislature to the provisions of any Bill or of subordinate legislation, which is in its opinion 'a differentiating measure' – that is to say, discriminatory – or is otherwise inconsistent with the fundamental liberties of the subject. Such a finding can be rejected by the legislature only by a two-thirds majority. In the United Kingdom, the Judicial Committee of the Privy Council has statutory competence to give an advisory opinion on any question of law referred to it; and it would be possible to refer a Parliamentary Bill to a suitably composed Judicial Committee for an opinion as to its consistency with the Bill of Rights. It would be for Parliament an opinion only, but it could perhaps be strengthened, as in Singapore, by a requirement of a special Parliamentary majority to enact the provisions of the Bill put in question by the opinion.

Another limited use of a Bill of Rights would be to make it the body of rules or standards to be applied by the Parliamentary Commissioners. Their fields of competence are being gradually extended, and it may be that in the longer term it is the Parliamentary Commissioner or Ombudsman system that is the most effective protection of basic rights, provided certain conditions are met. It would be at least necessary that the finding by the Parliamentary Commissioner was conclusive in the area of administration concerned, and that a needed change of practice, and reparation for the victim where appropriate, would necessarily follow, if the finding were that the action or practice was contrary to the Bill of Rights.

If however the Bill of Rights were to be made of general application, so as to cover the legislature, executive and judiciary, it would be primarily for the courts to make its application effective. And where proceedings in the courts themselves were called in question under the Bill, it would be for a higher court to determine whether it had been contravened. At least two general questions could arise for the Courts, as they have in the courts of countries that have incorporated the European Convention into domestic law. Are the Convention provisions applicable by the courts only to the extent that they are self-executing? Are the decisions and opinions of the Convention organs in Strasbourg binding or persuasive as to the interpretation of Convention provisions?

It is not surprising that divergent answers have been given to the first question in continental courts. The proposition that a Convention provision is not self-executing may be saying that further legislation is needed for its effective implementation because its terms are too broad or because such legislation was plainly envisaged by the drafters. Examples of the first might be 'Everyone has the right to . . . security of person/Toute personne a droit à la sûreté' (Article 5), and of the second the remedy provisions in Articles 5(5) and 13.

As regards the decisions and opinions of the Convention organs, the answer is, at least according to the practice in the majority of the Convention countries, that they are indicative or persuasive but not binding. The European Commission has rendered over eight thousand decisions, often containing elaborated interpretation of the Convention, the great mass of which are available to the public. The European Court has also delivered about thirty judgments.

It would add little to speculate here on the prospects of adoption of a new Bill of Rights for the United Kingdom. The decision is wholly political, and the contemporary attitude of many members of both major parties to European institutions does not suggest that at any rate the incorporation of the European Convention on Human Rights as domestic law will be undertaken. Some of the alternatives suggested above might then be perhaps considered.

APPENDIX

THE EUROPEAN CONVENTION FOR THE PROTECTION OF HUMAN RIGHTS AND FUNDAMENTAL FREEDOMS
(with amendments)[1]

The Governments signatory hereto, being Members of the Council of Europe;

Considering the Universal Declaration of Human Rights proclaimed by the General Assembly of the United Nations on 10th December 1948;

Considering that this Declaration aims at securing the universal and effective recognition and observance of the rights therein declared;

Considering that the aim of the Council of Europe is the achievement of greater unity between its Members and that one of the methods by which that aim is to be pursued is the maintenance and further realisation of human rights and fundamental freedoms;

Reaffirming their profound belief in those fundamental freedoms which are the foundation of justice and peace in the world and are best maintained on the one hand by an effective political democracy and on the other by a common understanding and observance of the human rights upon which they depend;

Being resolved, as the Governments of European countries which are like-minded and have a common heritage of political traditions, ideals, freedom and the rule of law, to take the first steps for the collective enforcement of certain of the rights stated in the Universal Declaration,

Have agreed as follows:

Article 1

The High Contracting Parties shall secure to everyone within their jurisdiction the rights and freedoms defined in Section 1 of this Convention.

SECTION I

Article 2

1 Everyone's right to life shall be protected by law. No one shall be deprived of his life intentionally save in the execution of a sentence of a court following his conviction of a crime for which this penalty is provided by law.

2 Deprivation of life shall not be regarded as inflicted in contravention of this article when it results from the use of force which is no more than absolutely necessary:

a in defence of any person from unlawful violence;

b in order to effect a lawful arrest or to prevent the escape of a person lawfully detained;

c in action lawfully taken for the purpose of quelling a riot or insurrection.

Article 3

No one shall be subjected to torture or to inhuman or degrading treatment or punishment.

Article 4

No one shall be held in slavery or servitude.

2 No one shall be required to perform forced or compulsory labour.

3 For the purpose of this article the term 'forced or compulsory labour' shall not include:

a any work required to be done in the ordinary course of detention imposed according to the provisions of Article 5 of this Convention or during conditional release from such detention;

b any service of a military character or, in case of conscientious objectors in countries where they are recognised, service exacted instead of compulsory military service;

c any service exacted in case of an emergency or calamity threatening the life or well-being of the community;

d any work or service which forms part of normal civic obligations.

Article 5

1 Everyone has the right to liberty and security of person. No

one shall be deprived of his liberty save in the following cases and in accordance with a procedure prescribed by law:

a the lawful detention of a person after conviction by a competent court;

b the lawful arrest or detention of a person for non-compliance with the lawful order of a court or in order to secure the fulfilment of any obligation prescribed by law;

c the lawful arrest or detention of a person effected for the purpose of bringing him before the competent legal authority on reasonable suspicion of having committed an offence or when it is reasonably considered necessary to prevent his committing an offence or fleeing after having done so;

d the detention of a minor by lawful order for the purpose of educational supervision or his lawful detention for the purpose of bringing him before the competent legal authority;

e the lawful detention of persons for the prevention of the spreading of infectious diseases, of persons of unsound mind, alcoholics or drug addicts or vagrants;

f the lawful arrest or detention of a person to prevent his effecting an unauthorised entry into the country or of a person against whom action is being taken with a view to deportation or extradition.

2 Everyone who is arrested shall be informed promptly, in a language which he understands, of the reasons for his arrest and of any charge against him.

3 Everyone arrested or detained in accordance with the provisions of paragraph 1.*c.* of this article shall be brought promptly before a judge or other officer authorised by law to exercise judicial power and shall be entitled to trial within a reasonable time or to release pending trial. Release may be conditioned by guarantees to appear for trial.

4 Everyone who is deprived of his liberty by arrest or detention shall be entitled to take proceedings by which the lawfulness of his detention shall be decided speedily by a court and his release ordered if the detention is not lawful.

5 Everyone who has been the victim of arrest or detention in contravention of the provisions of this article shall have an enforceable right to compensation.

Article 6

1   In the determination of his civil rights and obligations or of any criminal charge against him, everyone is entitled to a fair and public hearing within a reasonable time by an independent and impartial tribunal established by law. Judgement shall be pronounced publicly but the press and public may be excluded from all or part of the trial in the interests of morals, public order or national security in a democratic society, where the interests of juveniles or the protection of the private life of the parties so require, or to the extent strictly necessary in the opinion of the court in special circumstances where publicity would prejudice the interests of justice.

2   Everyone charged with a criminal offence shall be presumed innocent until proved guilty according to law.

3   Everyone charged with a criminal offence has the following minimum rights:

a to be informed promptly, in a language which he understands and in detail, of the nature and cause of the accusation against him;

b to have adequate time and facilities for the preparation of his defence;

c to defend himself in person or through legal assistance of his own choosing or, if he has not sufficient means to pay for legal assistance, to be given it free when the interests of justice so require;

d to examine or have examined witnesses against him and to obtain the attendance and examination of witnesses on his behalf under the same conditions as witnesses against him;

e to have the free assistance of an interpreter if he cannot understand or speak the language used in court.

Article 7

1   No one shall be held guilty of any criminal offence on account of any act or omission which did not constitute a criminal offence under national or international law at the time when it was committed. Nor shall a heavier penalty be imposed than the one that was applicable at the time the criminal offence was committed.

2   This article shall not prejudice the trial and punishment of any person for any act or omission which, at the time when it was

committed, was criminal according to the general principles of law recognised by civilised nations.

Article 8

1   Everyone has the right to respect for his private and family life, his home and his correspondence.

2   There shall be no interference by a public authority with the exercise of this right except such as is in accordance with the law and is necessary in a democratic society in the interests of national security, public safety or the economic well-being of the country, for the prevention of disorder or crime, for the protection of health or morals, or for the protection of the rights and freedoms of others.

Article 9

1   Everyone has the right to freedom of thought, conscience and religion; this right includes freedom to change his religion or belief and freedom, either alone or in community with others and in public or private, to manifest his religion or belief, in worship, teaching, practice and observance.

2   Freedom to manifest one's religion or beliefs shall be subject only to such limitations as are prescribed by law and are necessary in a democratic society in the interests of public safety, for the protection of public order, health or morals, or for the protection of the rights and freedoms of others.

Article 10

1   Everyone has the right to freedom of expression. This right shall include freedom to hold opinions and to receive and impart information and ideas without interference by public authority and regardless of frontiers. This article shall not prevent States from requiring the licensing of broadcasting, television or cinema enterprises.

2   The exercise of these freedoms, since it carries with it duties and responsibilities, may be subject to such formalities, conditions, restrictions or penalties as are prescribed by law and are necessary in a democratic society, in the interests of national security, territorial integrity or public safety, for the prevention of disorder or crime, for the protection of health or morals, for the protection of the reputation or rights of others, for preventing the

disclosure of information received in confidence, or for maintaining the authority and impartiality of the judiciary.

Article 11

1   Everyone has the right to freedom of peaceful assembly and to freedom of association with others, including the right to form and to join trade unions for the protection of his interests.

2   No restrictions shall be placed on the exercise of these rights other than such as are prescribed by law and are necessary in a democratic society in the interests of national security or public safety, for the prevention of disorder or crime, for the protection of health or morals or for the protection of the rights and freedoms of others. This article shall not prevent the imposition of lawful restrictions on the exercise of these rights by members of the armed forces, of the police or of the administration of the State.

Article 12

Men and women of marriageable age have the right to marry and to found a family, according to the national laws governing the exercise of this right.

Article 13

Everyone whose rights and freedoms as set forth in this Convention are violated shall have an effective remedy before a national authority notwithstanding that the violation has been committed by persons acting in an official capacity.

Article 14

The enjoyment of the rights and freedoms set forth in this Convention shall be secured without discrimination on any ground such as sex, race, colour, language, religion, political or other opinion, national or social origin, association with a national minority, property, birth or other status.

Article 15

1   In time of war or other public emergency threatening the life of the nation, any High Contracting Party may take measures derogating from its obligations under this Convention to the extent strictly required by the exigencies of the situation,

provided that such measures are not inconsistent with its other obligations under international law.

2   No derogation from Article 2, except in respect of deaths resulting from lawful acts of war, or from Articles 3, 4 (paragraph 1) and 7 shall be made under this provision.

3   Any High Contracting Party availing itself of this right of derogation shall keep the Secretary General of the Council of Europe fully informed of the measures which it has taken and the reasons therefor. It shall also inform the Secretary General of the Council of Europe when such measures have ceased to operate and the provisions of the Convention are again being fully executed.

Article 16

Nothing in Articles 10, 11 and 14 shall be regarded as preventing the High Contracting Parties from imposing restrictions on the political activity of aliens.

Article 17

Nothing in this Convention may be interpreted as implying for any State, group or person any right to engage in any activity or perform any act aimed at the destruction of any of the rights and freedoms set forth herein or at their limitation to a greater extent than is provided for in the Convention.

Article 18

The restrictions permitted under this Convention to the said rights and freedoms shall not be applied for any purpose other than those for which they have been prescribed.

SECTION II

Article 19

To ensure the observance of the engagements undertaken by the High Contracting Parties in the present Convention, there shall be set up:

a A European Commission of Human Rights, hereinafter referred to as 'the Commission';

b A European Court of Human Rights, hereinafter referred to as 'the Court'.

SECTION III

Article 20

The Commission shall consist of a number of members equal to that of the High Contracting Parties. No two members of the Commission may be nationals of the same State.

Article 21

1   The members of the Commission shall be elected by the Committee of Ministers by an absolute majority of votes, from a list of names drawn up by the Bureau of the Consultative Assembly; each group of the Representatives of the High Contracting Parties in the Consultative Assembly shall put forward three candidates, of whom two at least shall be its nationals.

2   As far as applicable, the same procedure shall be followed to complete the Commission in the event of other States subsequently becoming Parties to this Convention, and in filling casual vacancies.

Article 22

1   The members of the Commission shall be elected for a period of six years. They may be re-elected. However, of the members elected at the first election, the terms of seven members shall expire at the end of three years.

2   The members whose terms are to expire at the end of the initial period of three years shall be chosen by lot by the Secretary General of the Council of Europe immediately after the first election has been completed.

3   In order to ensure that, as far as possible, one half of the membership of the Commission shall be renewed every three years, the Committee of Ministers may decide, before proceeding to any subsequent election, that the term or terms of office of one or more members to be elected shall be for a period other than six years but not more than nine and not less than three years.

4   In cases where more than one term of office is involved and the Committee of Ministers applies the preceding paragraph, the allocation of the terms of office shall be effected by the drawing of lots by the Secretary General, immediately after the election.

5   A member of the Commission elected to replace a member

whose term of office has not expired shall hold office for the remainder of his predecessor's term.

6   The members of the Commission shall hold office until replaced. After having been replaced, they shall continue to deal with such cases as they already have under consideration.

Article 23

The members of the Commission shall sit on the Commission in their individual capacity.

Article 24

Any High Contracting Party may refer to the Commission, through the Secretary General of the Council of Europe, any alleged breach of the provisions of the Convention by another High Contracting Party.

Article 25

1   The Commission may receive petitions addressed to the Secretary General of the Council of Europe from any person, non-governmental organisation or group of individuals claiming to be the victim of a violation by one of the High Contracting Parties of the rights set forth in this Convention, provided that the High Contracting Party against which the complaint has been lodged has declared that it recognises the competence of the Commission to receive such petitions. Those of the High Contracting Parties who have made such a declaration undertake not to hinder in any way the effective exercise of this right.

2   Such declarations may be made for a specific period.

3   The declarations shall be deposited with the Secretary General of the Council of Europe who shall transmit copies thereof to the High Contracting Parties and publish them.

4   The Commission shall only exercise the powers provided for in this article when at least six High Contracting Parties are bound by declarations made in accordance with the preceding paragraphs.

Article 26

The Commission may only deal with the matter after all domestic remedies have been exhausted, according to the generally recognised rules of international law, and within a period of six months from the date on which the final decision was taken.

Article 27

1 The Commission shall not deal with any petition submitted under Article 25 which:

   a is anonymous, or

   b is substantially the same as a matter which has already been examined by the Commission or has already been submitted to another procedure of international investigation or settlement and if it contains no relevant new information.

2 The Commission shall consider inadmissible any petition submitted under Article 25 which it considers incompatible with the provisions of the present Convention, manifestly ill-founded, or an abuse of the right of petition.

3 The Commission shall reject any petition referred to it which it considers inadmissible under Article 26.

Article 28

In the event of the Commission accepting a petition referred to it:

   a it shall, with a view to ascertaining the facts, undertake together with the representatives of the parties an examination of the petition and, if need be, an investigation, for the effective conduct of which the States concerned shall furnish all necessary facilities, after an exchange of views with the Commission;

   b it shall place itself at the disposal of the parties concerned with a view to securing a friendly settlement of the matter on the basis of respect for human rights as defined in this Convention.

Article 29

After it has accepted a petition submitted under Article 25, the Commission may nevertheless decide unanimously to reject the petition if, in the course of its examination, it finds that the existence of one of the grounds for non-acceptance provided for in Article 27 has been established.

In such a case, the decision shall be communicated to the parties.

Article 30

If the Commission succeeds in effecting a friendly settlement in accordance with Article 28, it shall draw up a report which shall be sent to the States concerned, to the Committee of Ministers and to the Secretary General of the Council of Europe for publication. This report shall be confined to a brief statement of the facts and of the solution reached.

Article 31

1   If a solution is not reached, the Commission shall draw up a report on the facts and state its opinion as to whether the facts found disclose a breach by the State concerned of its obligations under the Convention. The opinions of all the members of the Commission on this point may be stated in the report.

2   The report shall be transmitted to the Committee of Ministers. It shall also be transmitted to the States concerned, who shall not be at liberty to publish it.

3   In transmitting the report to the Committee of Ministers the Commission may make such proposals as it thinks fit.

Article 32

1   If the question is not referred to the Court in accordance with Article 48 of this Convention within a period of three months from the date of the transmission of the report to the Committee of Ministers, the Committee of Ministers shall decide by a majority of two-thirds of the members entitled to sit on the Committee whether there has been a violation of the Convention.

2   In the affirmative case the Committee of Ministers shall prescribe a period during which the High Contracting Party concerned must take the measures required by the decision of the Committee of Ministers.

3   If the High Contracting Party concerned has not taken satisfactory measures within the prescribed period, the Committee of Ministers shall decide by the majority provided for in paragraph 1 above what effect shall be given to its original decision and shall publish the report.

4   The High Contracting Parties undertake to regard as binding on them any decision which the Committee of Ministers may take in application of the preceding paragraphs.

Article 33

The Commission shall meet *in camera*.

Article 34

Subject to the provisions of Article 29, the Commission shall take its decisions by a majority of the members present and voting.

Article 35

The Commission shall meet as the circumstances require. The meetings shall be convened by the Secretary General of the Council of Europe.

Article 36

The Commission shall draw up its own rules of procedure.

Article 37

The secretariat of the Commission shall be provided by the Secretary General of the Council of Europe.

SECTION IV

Article 38

The European Court of Human Rights shall consist of a number of judges equal to that of the Members of the Council of Europe. No two judges may be nationals of the same State.

Article 39

1   The members of the Court shall be elected by the Consultative Assembly by a majority of the votes cast from a list of persons nominated by the Members of the Council of Europe; each Member shall nominate three candidates, of whom two at least shall be its nationals.
2   As far as applicable, the same procedure shall be followed to complete the Court in the event of the admission of new Members of the Council of Europe, and in filling casual vacancies.
3   The candidates shall be of high moral character and must either possess the qualifications required for appointment to high

judicial office or be jurisconsults of recognised competence.

Article 40

1   The members of the Court shall be elected for a period of nine years. They may be re-elected. However, of the members elected at the first election the terms of four members shall expire at the end of three years, and the terms of four more members shall expire at the end of six years.

2   The members whose terms are to expire at the end of the initial periods of three and six years shall be chosen by lot by the Secretary General immediately after the first election has been completed.

3   In order to ensure that, as far as possible, one third of the membership of the Court shall be renewed every three years, the Consultative Assembly may decide, before proceeding to any subsequent election, that the term or terms of office of one or more members to be elected shall be for a period other than nine years but not more than twelve and not less than six years.

4   In cases where more than one term of office is involved and the Consultative Assembly applies the preceding paragraph, the allocation of the terms of office shall be effected by the drawing of lots by the Secretary General immediately after the election.

5   A member of the Court elected to replace a member whose term of office has not expired shall hold office for the remainder of his predecessor's term.

6   The members of the Court shall hold office until replaced. After having been replaced, they shall continue to deal with such cases as they already have under consideration.

Article 41

The Court shall elect its President and Vice-President for a period of three years. They may be re-elected.

Article 42

The members of the Court shall receive for each day of duty a compensation to be determined by the Committee of Ministers.

Article 43

For the consideration of each case brought before it the Court shall consist of a Chamber composed of seven judges. There shall sit as an *ex officio* member of the Chamber the judge who is a national of any State Party concerned, or, if there is none, a person of its choice who shall sit in the capacity of judge; the names of the other judges shall be chosen by lot by the President before the opening of the case.

Article 44

Only the High Contracting Parties and the Commission shall have the right to bring a case before the Court.

Article 45

The jurisdiction of the Court shall extend to all cases concerning the interpretation and application of the present Convention which the High Contracting Parties or the Commission shall refer to it in accordance with Article 48.

Article 46

1   Any of the High Contracting Parties may at any time declare that it recognises as compulsory *ipso facto* and without special agreement the jurisdiction of the Court in all matters concerning the interpretation and application of the present Convention.

2   The declarations referred to above may be made unconditionally or on condition of reciprocity on the part of several or certain other High Contracting Parties or for a specified period.

3   These declarations shall be deposited with the Secretary General of the Council of Europe who shall transmit copies thereof to the High Contracting Parties.

Article 47

The Court may only deal with a case after the Commission has acknowledged the failure of efforts for a friendly settlement and within the period of three months provided for in Article 32.

Article 48

The following may bring a case before the Court, provided that the High Contracting Party concerned, if there is only one, or the High Contracting Parties concerned, if there is more than one, are subject to the compulsory jurisdiction of the Court or, failing that, with the consent of the High Contracting Party concerned, if there is only one, or of the High Contracting Parties concerned if there is more than one:

   a the Commission;

   b a High Contracting Party whose national is alleged to be a victim;

   c a High Contracting Party which referred the case to the Commission;

   d a High Contracting Party against which the complaint has been lodged.

Article 49

In the event of dispute as to whether the Court has juris diction, the matter shall be settled by the decision of the Court.

Article 50

If the Court finds that a decision or a measure taken by a legal authority or any other authority of a High Contracting Party is completely or partially in conflict with the obligations arising from the present Convention, and if the internal law of the said Party allows only partial reparation to be made for the consequences of this decision or measure, the decision of the Court shall, if necessary, afford just satisfaction to the injured party.

Article 51

1   Reasons shall be given for the judgment of the Court.

2   If the judgment does not represent in whole or in part the unanimous opinion of the judges, any judge shall be entitled to deliver a separate opinion.

Article 52

The judgment of the Court shall be final.

Article 53

The High Contracting Parties undertake to abide by the decision of the Court in any case to which they are parties.

Article 54

The judgment of the Court shall be transmitted to the Committee of Ministers which shall supervise its execution.

Article 55

The Court shall draw up its own rules and shall determine its own procedure.

Article 56

1 The first election of the members of the Court shall take place after the declarations by the High Contracting Parties mentioned in Article 46 have reached a total of eight.
2 No case can be brought before the Court before this election.

SECTION V

Article 57

On receipt of a request from the Secretary General of the Council of Europe any High Contracting Party shall furnish an explanation of the manner in which its internal law ensures the effective implementation of any of the provisions of this Convention.

Article 58

The expenses of the Commission and the Court shall be borne by the Council of Europe.

Article 59

The members of the Commission and of the Court shall be entitled, during the discharge of their functions, to the privileges and immunities provided for in Article 40 of the Statute of the Council of Europe and in the agreements made thereunder.

Article 60

Nothing in this Convention shall be construed as limiting or derogating from any of the human rights and fundamental freedoms which may be ensured under the laws of any High Contracting Party or under any other agreement to which it is a Party.

Article 61

Nothing in this Convention shall prejudice the powers conferred on the Committee of Ministers by the Statute of the Council of Europe.

Article 62

The High Contracting Parties agree that, except by special agreement, they will not avail themselves of treaties, conventions or declarations in force between them for the purpose of submitting, by way of petition, a dispute arising out of the interpretation or application of this Convention to a means of settlement other than those provided for in this Convention.

Article 63

1 Any State may at the time of its ratification or at any time thereafter declare by notification addressed to the Secretary General of the Council of Europe that the present Convention shall extend to all or any of the territories for whose international relations it is responsible.

2 The Convention shall extend to the territory or territories named in the notification as from the thirtieth day after the receipt of this notification by the Secretary General of the Council of Europe.

3 The provisions of this Convention shall be applied in such territories with due regard, however, to local requirements.

4 Any State which has made a declaration in accordance with paragraph 1 of this article may at any time thereafter declare on behalf of one or more of the territories to which the declaration relates that it accepts the competence of the Commission to receive petitions from individuals, non-governmental organisations or groups of individuals in accordance with Article 25 of the present Convention.

Article 64

1 Any State may, when signing this Convention or when depositing its instrument of ratification, make a reservation in respect of any particular provision of the Convention to the extent that any law then in force in its territory is not in conformity with the provision. Reservations of a general character shall not be permitted under this article.

2 Any reservation made under this article shall contain a brief statement of the law concerned.

Article 65

1   A High Contracting Party may denounce the present Convention only after the expiry of five years from the date on which it became a Party to it and after six months' notice contained in a notification addressed to the Secretary General of the Council of Europe, who shall inform the other High Contracting Parties.

2   Such a denunciation shall not have the effect of releasing the High Contracting Party concerned from its obligations under this Convention in respect of any act which, being capable of constituting a violation of such obligations, may have been performed by it before the date at which the denunciation became effective.

3   Any High Contracting Party which shall cease to be a Member of the Council of Europe shall cease to be a Party to this Convention under the same conditions.

4   The Convention may be denounced in accordance with the provisions of the preceding paragraphs in respect of any territory to which it has been declared to extend under the terms of Article 63.

Article 66

1   This Convention shall be open to the signature of the Members of the Council of Europe. It shall be ratified. Ratifications shall be deposited with the Secretary General of the Council of Europe.

2   The present Convention shall come into force after the deposit of ten instruments of ratification.

3   As regards any signatory ratifying subsequently, the Convention shall come into force at the date of the deposit of its instrument of ratification.

4   The Secretary General of the Council of Europe shall notify all the Members of the Council of Europe of the entry into force of the Convention, the names of the High Contracting Parties who have ratified it, and the deposit of all instruments of ratification which may be effected subsequently.

FIRST PROTOCOL TO THE CONVENTION

The Governments signatory hereto, being Members of the Council of Europe,

Being resolved to take steps to ensure the collective enforcement of certain rights and freedoms other than those already included in Section I of the Convention for the Protection of Human Rights and Fundamental Freedoms signed at Rome on 4th November, 1950 (hereinafter referred to as 'the Convention'),

Have agreed as follows:

Article 1

Every natural or legal person is entitled to the peaceful enjoyment of his possessions. No one shall be deprived of his possessions except in the public interest and subject to the conditions provided for by law and by the general principles of international law.

The preceding provisions shall not, however, in any way impair the right of a State to enforce such laws as it deems necessary to control the use of property in accordance with the general interest or to secure the payment of taxes or other contributions or penalties.

Article 2

No person shall be denied the right to education. In the exercise of any functions which it assumes in relation to education and to teaching, the State shall respect the right of parents to ensure such education and teaching in conformity with their own religious and philosophical convictions.

Article 3

The High Contracting Parties undertake to hold free elections at reasonable intervals by secret ballot, under conditions which will ensure the free expression of the opinion of the people in the choice of the legislature.

Article 4

Any High Contracting Party may at the time of signature or ratification or at any time thereafter communicate to the Secretary General of the Council of Europe a declaration stating the extent to which it undertakes that the provisions of the present Protocol shall apply to such of the territories for the international relations of which it is responsible as are named therein.

Any High Contracting Party which has communicated a declaration in virtue of the preceding paragraph may from time to time communicate a further declaration modifying the terms of any former declaration or terminating the application of the provisions of this Protocol in respect of any territory.

A declaration made in accordance with this article shall be deemed to have been made in accordance with paragraph 1 of Article 63 of the Convention.

Article 5

As between the High Contracting Parties the provisions of Articles 1, 2, 3 and 4 of this Protocol shall be regarded as additional articles to the Convention and all the provisions of the Convention shall apply accordingly.

Article 6

This Protocol shall be open for signature by the Members of the Council of Europe, who are the signatories of the Convention; it shall be ratified at the same time as or after the ratification of the Convention. It shall enter into force after the deposit of ten instruments of ratification. As regards any signatory ratifying subsequently, the Protocol shall enter into force at the date of the deposit of its instrument of ratification.

The instruments of ratification shall be deposited with the Secretary General of the Council of Europe, who will notify all Members of the names of those who have ratified.

SECOND PROTOCOL TO THE CONVENTION
conferring upon the European Court of Human Rights competence to give advisory opinions.

The Member States of the Council of Europe signatory hereto:
Having regard to the provisions of the Convention for the Protection of Human Rights and Fundamental Freedoms signed

at Rome on 4th November 1950 (hereinafter referred to as 'the Convention') and, in particular, Article 19 instituting, among other bodies, a European Court of Human Rights (hereinafter referred to as 'the Court');

Considering that it is expedient to confer upon the Court competence to give advisory opinions subject to certain conditions;

Have agreed as follows:

Article 1

1 The Court may, at the request of the Committee of Ministers, give advisory opinions on legal questions concerning the interpretation of the Convention and the Protocols thereto.

2 Such opinions shall not deal with any question relating to the content or scope of the rights or freedoms defined in Section I of the Convention and in the Protocols thereto, or with any other question which the Commission, the Court or the Committee of Ministers might have to consider in consequence of any such proceedings as could be instituted in accordance with the Convention.

3 Decisions of the Committee of Ministers to request an advisory opinion of the Court shall require a two-thirds majority vote of the representatives entitled to sit on the Committee.

Article 2

The Court shall decide whether a request for an advisory opinion submitted by the Committee of Ministers is within its consultative competence as defined in Article 1 of this Protocol.

Article 3

1 For the consideration of requests for an advisory opinion, the Court shall sit in plenary session.

2 Reasons shall be given for advisory opinions of the Court.

3 If the advisory opinion does not represent in whole or in part the unanimous opinion of the judges, any judge shall be entitled to deliver a separate opinion.

4 Advisory opinions of the Court shall be communicated to the Committee of Ministers.

Article 4

The powers of the Court under Article 55 of the Convention

shall extend to the drawing up of such rules and the determination of such procedure as the Court may think necessary for the purposes of this Protocol.

Article 5

1 This Protocol shall be open to signature by member States of the Council of Europe, signatories to the Convention, who may become Parties to it by:

a signature without reservation in respect of ratification or acceptance;

b signature with reservation in respect of ratification or acceptance, followed by ratification or accpetance.

Instruments of ratification or acceptance shall be deposited with the Secretary General of the Council of Europe.

2 This Protocol shall enter into force as soon as all States Parties to the Convention shall have become Parties to the Protocol, in accordance with the provisions of paragraph 1 of this article.

3 From the date of the entry into force of this Protocol, Articles 1 to 4 shall be considered an integral part of the Convention.

4 The Secretary General of the Council of Europe shall notify the member States of the Council of:

a any signature without reservation in respect of ratification or acceptance;

b any signature with reservation in respect of ratification or acceptance;

c the deposit of any instrument of ratification or acceptance;

d the date of entry into force of this Protocol in accordance with paragraph 2 of this article.

FOURTH PROTOCOL TO THE CONVENTION
securing certain rights and freedoms other than those already included in the Convention and in the first Protocol thereto.

The Governments signatory hereto, being Members of the Council of Europe,

Being resolved to take steps to ensure the collective enforcement of certain rights and freedoms other than those already included in Section I of the Convention for the Protection of Human Rights and Fundamental Freedoms signed at Rome on 4th November 1950 (hereinafter referred to as 'the Convention') and in Articles 1 to 3 of the first Protocol to the Convention, signed at Paris on 20th March 1952,

Have agreed as follows:

Article 1

No one shall be deprived of his liberty merely on the ground of inability to fulfil a contractual obligation.

Article 2

1   Everyone lawfully within the territory of a State shall, within that territory, have the right to liberty of movement and freedom to choose his residence.

2   Everyone shall be free to leave any country, including his own.

3   No restrictions shall be placed on the exercise of these rights other than such as are in accordance with law and are necessary in a democratic society in the interests of national security or public safety, for the maintenance of *ordre public*, for the prevention of crime, for the protection of health or morals, or for the protection of the rights and freedoms of others.

4   The rights set forth in paragraph 1 may also be subject, in particular areas, to restrictions imposed in accordance with law and justified by the public interest in a democratic society.

Article 3

1   No one shall be expelled, by means either of an individual or of a collective measure, from the territory of the State of which he is a national.

2   No one shall be deprived of the right to enter the territory of the State of which he is a national.

Article 4

Collective expulsion of aliens is prohibited.

Article 5

1   Any High Contracting Party may, at the time of signature or ratification of this Protocol, or at any time thereafter, communicate to the Secretary General of the Council of Europe a declaration stating the extent to which it undertakes that the provisions of this Protocol shall apply to such of the territories for the international relations of which it is responsible as are named therein.

2   Any High Contracting Party which has communicated a declaration in virtue of the preceding paragraph may, from time to time, communicate a further declaration modifying the terms of any former declaration or terminating the application of the provisions of this Protocol in respect of any territory.

3   A declaration made in accordance with this article shall be deemed to have been made in accordance with paragraph 1 of Article 63 of the Convention.

4   The territory of any State to which this Protocol applies by virtue of ratification or acceptance by that State, and each territory to which this Protocol is applied by virtue of a declaration by that State under this article, shall be treated as separate territories for the purpose of the references in Articles 2 and 3 to the territory of a State.

Article 6

1   As between the High Contracting Parties the provisions of Articles 1 to 5 of this Protocol shall be regarded as additional articles to the Convention, and all the provisions of the Convention shall apply accordingly.

2   Nevertheless, the right of individual recourse recognised by a declaration made under Article 25 of the Convention, or the acceptance of the compulsory jurisdiction of the Court by a declaration made under Article 46 of the Convention, shall not be effective in relation to this Protocol unless the High Contracting Party concerned has made a statement recognising such right, or accepting such jurisdiction, in respect of all or any of Articles 1 to 4 of the Protocol.

Article 7

1   This Protocol shall be open for signature by the Members of the Council of Europe who are the signatories of the Convention;

it shall be ratified at the same time as or after the ratification of the Convention. It shall enter into force after the deposit of five instruments of ratification. As regards any signatory ratifying subsequently, the Protocol shall enter into force at the date of the deposit of its instrument of ratification.

2   The instruments of ratification shall be depositied with the Secretary General of the Council of Europe, who will notify all Members of the names of those who have ratified.

SAMPLE NOTICES OF DEROGATION

'The United Kingdom Permanent Representative to the Council of Europe presents his compliments to the Secretary General of the Council, and has the honour to convey the following information in order to ensure compliance with the obligations of Her Majesty's Government in the United Kingdom under Article 15(3) of the Convention for the Protection of Human Rights and Fundamental Freedoms signed at Rome on 4 November 1950.

A public emergency within the meaning of Article 15(1) of the Convention exists in a part of the United Kingdom, namely, Northern Ireland.

Owing to the recurrence in Northern Ireland of organised terrorism, certain emergency powers have been brought into operation at various dates between 16 June 1954, and 11 January 1957, in order to preserve the peace and prevent outbreaks of violence, loss of life and damage to property; for these purposes the Government of Northern Ireland, to the extent strictly required by the exigencies of the situation have exercised powers to detain persons, to search and seize, and to prohibit the publication and distribution of certain printed matter, which may involve derogations in certain respects from the obligations imposed by the Convention for the Protection of Human Rights and Fundamental Freedoms.'

27 June 1957

'The United Kingdom Permanent Representative to the Council of Europe presents his compliments to the Secretary General of the Council of Europe and has the honour to refer to the communication of 20 August 1971 in which he informed the Secretary General, pursuant to Article 15 of the Convention, of the exercise of certain powers of detention and internment for the protection of life and the security of property and to prevent the outbreaks of public disorder in Northern Ireland. Subsequently copies of relevant legislation, being regulations under the Civil Authorities (Special Powers) Act (Northern Ireland) 1922, were sent to the Secretary General.

On 1 November 1972 an Order was made under the Northern Ireland (Temporary Provisions) Act 1972 which revoked certain of the regulations under the Act of 1922 and made new provision in their place. This Order, the Detention of Terrorists (Northern Ireland) Order 1972, has been approved by both Houses of Parliament. It was approved by the House of Lords on 7 December 1972 and the House of Commons on 11 December 1972. Under the new provisions a person can be detained if it is shown to the satisfaction of a legally qualified Commissioner that the person in question has been concerned in the commission or attempted commission of an act of terrorism or the direction, organization or training of persons for the purpose of terrorism and (in any such case) his detention is necessary for the protection of the public. Provision is made for an appeal against any order for detention made by a Commissioner. Six copies of the orders are enclosed herewith.

The United Kingdom Permanent Representative avails himself of this opportunity to renew to the Secretary General the assurance of his highest consideration.'

23 January 1973

REFERENCES

1 HUMAN RIGHTS: THE CURRENT SITUATION: *Lord Scarman*

1 House of Commons Paper 433
2 Cmnd. 7009 (1977) London
3 *A.-G. v. Times Newspapers* [1974] A.C. 273
4 Cf. *Report of the Committee on Contempt of Court.* Cmnd. 5794 (1974) London
5 Quoted by Judge Zekia in his separate opinion: *Sunday Times* case, *loc. cit.* at p. 65
6 And cf. Professor Fawcett's article below at p. 000
7 Judgment of Court of Human Rights, 21 February 1975
8 Judgment of Court of Human Rights, 18 January 1978
9 Judgment of Court of Human Rights, 6 September 1978

3 INTRODUCING A BILL OF RIGHTS: *Lord Wade*

1 *Report of the Select Committee on a Bill of Rights.* House of Lords paper 176 (1978)

4 ARGUMENTS AGAINST A BILL OF RIGHTS: *Lord Boston of Faversham*

1 *Report of the Select Committee on a Bill of Rights* House of Lords paper 176 (1978) at p. 20.
2 I do not suggest such provisions might not be better covered through general legislation – that is another matter.
3 Parliamentary Debates (H of L) Vol. 396 Cols 1373-4
4 *Op. cit.* Col. 1364 *et seq.*
5 *Op. cit.*
6 *Loc. cit.* at p. 32
7 Parliamentary Debates (H of L) *op. cit.* Cols. 1375-6
8 *Minutes of Evidence taken before the Select Committee on a Bill of Rights* HMSO (81) p. 228
9 Parliamentary Debates (H of L) *op. cit.* Col. 1367
10 *Op. cit.* Cols. 1389 *et seq.*
11 *Loc. sit.* pp. 33-4

12   Parliamentary Debates (H of L) Vol. 379 Cols. 1011-1012

5   WHAT DOES A BILL OF RIGHTS MEAN IN PRACTICE? *Professor Peter Wallington*

1   Wallington and McBride: *Civil Liberties and a Bill of Rights* 1976 Cobden Trust, London
2   In fact the new immigration regulations were not introduced by statute but this need not affect the validity of this hypothetical example.
3   *Ireland v. U.K.* Judgment of the Court of Human Rights 18 January 1978
4   *Report of the Committee on Contempt of Court* Cmnd. 5794 (1974) London

6   THE PROTECTION OF HUMAN RIGHTS IN THE REPUBLIC OF IRELAND: *Senator Mary Robinson*

1   J.M. Kelly 'The Irish Constitution' Jurist Publishing Co. Ltd., University College Dublin, 1980
2   J.M. Kelly 'Fundamental Rights in the Irish Law and Constitution' 2nd Ed. at p. 16 Allen Figgis & Co. Ltd., 1967
3   The Emergency Powers Bill 1976 was referred to the Supreme Court and found to be constitutional: see below.
4   *The State (Quinn) v. Ryan* (1965) IR at p. 126
5   'Personal Rights under the Irish Constitution' *Irish Jurist,* Vol. XI New Series Part II, 205-222
6   *The State (Healy) v. Donoghue* (1976) IR 325 at 347
7   Cf. for example *McDonald v. Bord na gCon* (1965) IR 217; *East Donegal Co-op v. A.G.* (1970) IR 317; In *re Haughey* (1971) IR 217
8   (1965) IR 294
9   *Loc. cit.* at p. 211
10   D.G. Morgan: 'Court's Risky New Powers' *Irish Times* 6/7 February 1980
11   In *Re Article 26 and the Emergency Powers Bill 1976* (1977) IR 159
12   *Lawless v. Ireland,* Judgment of Court of Human Rights, July 1961, para. 30
13   An amendment was introduced during the Bill's passage through the Oireachtas so that the sub-section relating to the

belief of the Chief Superintendent would remain in force only so long as Part 5 of the Act of 1939 is in force.

14   Mr Paddy Cooney, 85 Seanad Debates, 31 August 1976, Column 13
15   M.P.O'Boyle: 'Emergency Situations and the Protection of Human Rights' Vol. 28 *NILQ* 1977 at p. 164
16   This section is based on my article 'The Special Criminal Court – Eight Years On' *Fortnight*, Issue No. 125, March 1980
17   'The Special Criminal Court', Dublin Univ. Press, 1974
18   Detailed figures are contained in *Fortnight loc. cit.*
19   *The Irish Times*, 15 October 1977
20   Report of the Committee on the Constitution, December 1967 (Pr. 9817)
21   *McGee v. Attorney General* (1974) IR 284
22   *G. v. Adoption Board*, 113 ILTR 25
23   (1974) IR 284
24   See above p. 53
25   The four Private Members' Bills were introduced by the author alone or with other senators.
26   *Irish Family Planning Association v. Judge Ryan* (Unreported)
27   *Murphy v. A.G.* (Unreported) 1980
28   *Mulloy v. Minister for Education* (1975) IR 88
29   *M. v. An Bord Uchtala* (1975) IR 81
30   *McGrath & O'Ruairc v. Trustees of Maynooth College* (Unreported 1979)
31   (1966) IR 567
32   See above p. 71
33   *Airey v. Ireland*, Judgment of Court of Human Rights 9th October 1979

7   VIOLENCE AND HUMAN RIGHTS IN NORTHERN IRELAND

1   *Ireland v. United Kingdom* Judgment of the European Court of Human Rights 18 January 1978
2   Cmnd. 7009 London (1977)
3   Review of the Operation of the Prevention of Terrorism (Temporary Provisions) Acts 1974 and 1976 Cmnd. 7324 London (1978)

4   Fifth Report of the Standing Advisory Commission on Human Rights Annual Report for 1978-79 House of Commons Paper 433
5   *Op. cit.*
6   (1978) 7 *NIJB* and cf. (1980) 1 *All ER* 166
7   *Loc. cit.*
8   *Op. cit.* at para. 2.06
9   *Law and State: The Case of Northern Ireland* Martin Robertson 1975; 'Emergency Power: Ten Years On' *Fortnight* Issue No. 125
10   *Loc. cit.*
11   *Op. cit.* at para. 6.15
12   'Report of a Committee to consider in the context of civil liberties and human rights measures to deal with terrorism in Northern Ireland' Cmnd. 5847 London (1975)

8   THE EUROPEAN CONVENTION IN OPERATION: *John Smythe*

1   *Airey v. Ireland* Judgment of the Court of Human Rights 9 October 1979
2   H.C. Deb. 14 January 1980 Col. 624
3   *Golder v. United Kingdom* Judgement of the Court of Human Rights 21 February 1975
4   *Belgian Linguistics Case*, Judgement of the Court of Human Rights 23 July 1968
5   *Handyside Case*, Judgement of the Court of Human Rights 7 December 1976
6   *Lawless v. Ireland* Vol. 4 Yearbook of European Convention on Human Rights
7   *Greek Case*, Vol. 12 Yearbook of European Convention on Human Rights

9   ACCESSION OF THE EUROPEAN COMMUNITY TO THE EUROPEAN CONVENTION ON HUMAN RIGHTS: *Dr C.-D. Ehlermann*

1   Legally speaking, there are three distinct Communities – the ECSC (European Coal and Steel Community), the EEC (the

European Economic Community), and Euratom – but it is usual to refer to them, whenever possible, by the expression Community.

2   *Stork v. High Authority* [1959] ECR, p. 17
3   *Stauder v. City of Ulm* [1969] ECR, p. 491. Internationale Handelsgesellschaft [1970] ECR, p. 1125
4   *Nold v. Commission* [1974] ECR, p. 491
5   *Hauer v. Land Rheinland-Pfalz*, 13 December 1979, not yet reported
6   *Stauder v. City of Ulm, supra.*
7   *Rutili v. Minister for the Interior* [1975] ECR, p. 1219
8   *Prais v. Council* [1976] ECR, p. 1589
9   *Hauer v. Land Rheinland-Pfalz, supra.*
10   Judgment of 28 May 1974, BVerfGE 37, 271
11   Judgment of 27 December 1973, Foro Italiano, 1974, I 315; Giurisprudenza Italiana, 1974, I, 1 865 – Giurisprudenza Costituzionale, 1973, 2406
12   OJ C No 127, 21 May 1979, p. 69
13   Bulletin of the European Communities, Supplement 5/76
14   OJ C 103 of 27 April 1977
15   OJ C No 39, 18 January 1979, p. 47
16   Bulletin of the European Communities 3 – 1978
17   Bulletin of the European Communities, Supplement 2/79
18   Articles 1-12, 14, 16-18 of the Convention, Articles 1-3 of the First Protocol, and Articles 1-4 of the Fourth Protocol.
19   Referred to above p. 118
20   *Hugin v. Commission* [1979] ECR, p. 1869
21   See above p. 116
22   See the Prais case above p. 116
23   Codified version OJ C 189, p. 43, of 1975
24   OJ C No. 325, 29th December 1979, p. 10
25   See above p. 117
26   *CFDT v. The European Communities*, alternatively their Member States
27   See above p. 119

10   BILLS OF RIGHTS: SOME ALTERNATIVES:
Professor J. E. S. Fawcett

1   The use of special majorities is mentioned below.
2   The countries which have *not* incorporated are Iceland,

Norway, Sweden, Denmark, Ireland, United Kingdom and Malta.

APPENDIX

1   Grateful acknowledgement is given to the Council of Europe for permission to reprint the Convention and Protocols.